Collins *gem*

Garden Birds

Stephen Moss

HarperCollinsPublishers
1 London Bridge Street
London, SE1 9GF

www.harpercollins.co.uk

HarperCollins*Publishers*
Macken House, 39/40 Mayor Street Upper,
Dublin 1 D01 C9W8, Ireland

Collins is a registered trademark of
HarperCollinsPublishers Ltd.

First published in 2004
This edition published 2021

20

A catalogue record for this book is available from the British Library.

ISBN-13: 978 0 00 717614 4

Designed by Penny Dawes

Printed in India by Replika Press Pvt. Ltd.

MIX
Paper | Supporting
responsible forestry
FSC™ C007454

CONTENTS

Contents

INTRODUCTION

Watching birds in our gardens, parks and towns is not only a great pleasure and delight, it also helps you take the first steps on the road to becoming a 'proper' birdwatcher. Most town and garden birds are fairly tame and used to living alongside human beings, so will generally allow you to approach closely enough to see the details of their plumage and behaviour.

In addition, in recent years there has been a boom in garden bird feeding, so that there are plenty of different foods and feeders on offer to help you attract the widest possible variety of birds to your garden.

Canada Geese

salmonella. Removing surplus food at the end of each day also avoids attracting pests.

If you can, buy food from approved dealers. It is generally better to avoid peanuts or seed sold in outlets such as pet shops and garden centres, as they may not be suitable.

Food for feeders

Until relatively recently, the only alternative to peanuts was 'birdseed', a rather dubious mixture of various seeds and grains. Today, however, the wildbird food trade provides an extraordinary variety of seeds designed to attract particular species.

It is best to buy both peanuts and seeds in fairly small quantities, ensuring a rapid turnover. If you do need to store food for longer periods, make sure it is kept in secure bags in a cool, dry place.

Many birds, including Robins, Dunnocks, Starlings and Jays, prefer to eat live food such as insects and other invertebrates. A good substitute for natural foods is mealworms, which should be placed in a smooth-sided bowl to prevent escape.

NEST SITES

There are two main ways in which we can provide nest sites for our garden birds. First, by planting the right variety of bushes and shrubs in which they can safely nest; second, by providing artificial nest sites in the form of nestboxes.

Planting for nesting birds
Even in the smallest city plot there is room for a couple of dense shrubs in which a pair of Robins can build their nest; or a small area of scrubby bushes suitable for Wrens or Dunnocks.

If your garden is larger, there is plenty of scope for providing opportunities for breeding. Popular garden shrubs such as Clematis or Berberis are ideal for Blackbirds. Native plants such as Elder and Hawthorn provide nest sites for a wide range of garden birds, or try letting part of your garden 'go wild' by planting Bramble bushes.

Nestboxes
A good quality, well sited nestbox offers all the advantages of a natural nest site, and also allows us to enjoy the privilege of watching the intimate details of

Blackcap

breeding behaviour from the comfort of our kitchen window.

When buying a nestbox, it's generally best to avoid over fancy designs such as those often sold as ornaments in garden centres. Where nesting birds are concerned, form and function are far more important than style. So buy your nestbox from a reputable source such as the RSPB or one of the leading bird food suppliers.

Nestbox designs

There are two main designs:
● The 'tit box': a rectangular design with a small hole in the front to allow hole-nesting species such as Blue and Great Tits, House and Tree Sparrows, or Nuthatch, depending on the size of the entrance hole.

● The open-fronted box: a similar design, but with a large rectangular opening at the front, suitable for species such as Robin, Pied Wagtail and Spotted Flycatcher.

More specialised nestboxes can also be made, including those for House Martin or Treecreeper, or larger birds such as Kestrel or Barn Owl.

Siting a nestbox

The basic rules for siting a nestbox are:

● put the box in place during the autumn or early winter, to give the birds the chance to get used to it.

● fix the box somewhere solid, such as a sturdy garden fence, wall or post; between one-and-a-half

A tit nestbox in an urban garden

Nest of Blue Tits

and five metres above the ground.
● avoid siting the box where it will receive direct sunlight during the hottest part of the day.
● strike a balance between a site to which the birds can gain easy access, using suitable perches; and one which predators such as cats can reach.

Once the box is in place, you need to resist the temptation to inspect the box constantly, as this may disturb the nesting birds and make them desert. After the breeding season is over, you may open the box, remove any nesting material, unhatched eggs or dead young, and give the box a thorough clean.

WATER FOR BIRDS

Water for drinking

Without a regular supply of clean drinking water, birds will dehydrate, especially during hot summer weather. When taking a drink, birds are very vulnerable to attack by predators such as cats or Sparrowhawks, so most birds drink quickly and cautiously, often arriving and leaving in small flocks to minimise the chance of being caught.

Water for bathing

Regular bathing is also vital, as it allows birds to keep their plumage clean and fresh. Many birds bathe at least once a day, often in the morning or evening. By providing a regular source of clean water, we save the birds the time and trouble of seeking out natural alternatives. During the winter, when they need to feed almost constantly in order to survive, this can make a real difference to their chances of survival.

Bird baths

Next to a bird table, the bird bath is one of the most essential pieces of equipment for garden birds.

● avoid fancy ornamental designs sold in garden centres, as they may be unsuitable, especially for smaller birds, which require a well-designed bath.

● make sure your bath is sturdy and solid, with a gentle gradient from shallow to deeper water to allow different sized birds to drink and bathe at the same time.

● make sure the surface of the bath is not too smooth, as birds' feet may slip on it.

● make sure the design enables you to refill the bath with clean water once a day, and also allows you to clean it easily.

● pay particular attention to hygiene, especially during hot weather in summer, when bacteria can build up very rapidly, spreading disease amongst the birds.

Starling

Garden ponds

Garden ponds can help garden birds in several ways. First, by providing a place to drink and bathe, as an alternative to streams, lakes or bird baths. Second, by increasing the variety of insect and invertebrate life in your garden, which in turn provides an important food resource for the birds.

From a broader perspective, garden ponds are vital oases for all kinds of other natural creatures, especially frogs and newts, which are becoming ever scarcer as their natural habitat disappears.

Pond maintenance and safety

Be prepared to devote time to regular maintenance of your pond, although once it is well established this shouldn't involve all that much work. Important aspects include:

- removing fallen leaves during the autumn to avoid blocking light into the pond.
- during hot weather or prolonged droughts, clearing algae off the surface of your pond; and occasionally topping up the water level if things get really dry.
- in harsh winter weather, breaking or melting surface ice.

Finally, if there are likely to be small children between the ages of one and four in your garden, make sure that they cannot get access to your pond.

PESTS AND PREDATORS

Predators and pests come in all shapes and sizes, be they cats or squirrels, Sparrowhawks or Magpies, or the unseen rodent visitors that eat spilled food each night after the birds have gone to roost.

Dealing with these creatures requires the right attitude of mind, in which a certain level of nuisance is considered acceptable, but attempts are made to reduce the worst excesses. No garden is ever going to be completely free from pests and predators, but you can take steps to keep them in check.

Cats

Cats are a major problem for several reasons. The first, and most obvious, is that they are not a natural part of the birds' environment, so like any introduced predator they have a disproportionate effect on populations of natural wildlife. Because we feed and shelter them, they have another unfair advantage over wild birds.

One simple way to reduce the death toll is to make sure your cat wears a bell, which is supposed to warn birds of its approach. Another solution is to use a cat deterrent. These machines emit a high-pitched sound inaudible

Cat as predator

to the human ear but intolerable to cats, which then make sure they give your garden a wide berth!

Squirrels

The Grey Squirrel's ability to climb, combined with sharp claws and a very healthy appetite, makes it difficult to deter them. You can buy squirrel-proof feeders, which use a system of closely-spaced metal bars designed to let the small birds in to feed while excluding the larger squirrels. These do work, although may spoil your enjoyment as you watch the feeding birds.

Bird predators

In gardens there are two main species of bird predator: the Sparrowhawk and Magpie. Despite newspaper headlines claiming that the Magpie presents the greatest threat to our garden birds, research has shown that the worrying falls in population are largely a result of modern farming methods.

Since the banning of harmful pesticides, Sparrowhawks have become especially common in leafy, wooded suburbs, towns and city centres. However, their ability to conceal themselves in foliage, and habit of flying rapidly from place to place, means that they are not seen as often as you might expect.

Red Squirrel

Other pests

Many gardeners spend their time battling against a legion of pests, including aphids, slugs and caterpillars. Much of the damage these creatures do is purely cosmetic, by spoiling the foliage of flowering plants as they feed on it.

You can use pesticides to control them, but these can be harmful to humans and domestic animals as well as birds, so it is best to avoid them. Far better to encourage the widest variety of natural predators, such as ladybirds, which eat aphids; Song Thrushes, which feed on slugs and snails; and other small birds which feed their young on caterpillars.

CHANGES TO GARDEN BIRDS

It is easy to assume that garden birds are immune to any major changes that might affect the populations, range or distribution of birds in the wider countryside. But like any bird species, garden birds lead complex lives, in which food supply, changes in habitat and land use, and more global factors such as climate change, all play their part.

In recent years several formerly common, widespread and familiar species – many of which we simply took for granted – have suffered rapid and sometimes severe declines. For example the House Sparrow, once a bird so common we mostly ignored it, has undergone a population crash of at least 50 per cent in less than 30 years. The Starling, too, is in decline, and we rarely see those huge roosts that were once found in most large towns and cities. Even the Song Thrush has disappeared from many former haunts.

The blame for these declines cannot be put on a single cause, though there is little doubt that modern farming methods, which leave little or no waste seed on the ground after harvest, kill insects with pesticides, and have destroyed hedges and drained ponds, are

Starling

responsible for many of the problems. These changes affect garden birds because they have reduced the amount of food available, and therefore reduced bird populations as a whole.

Other changes in land use, such as building development and the rapid spread of the road network, also affect our birds; either by destroying or fragmenting habitat, or by reducing the population of insects on which they feed. This is why gardens are so important: they provide a vital oasis of habitat which birds can rely on, as well as a steady supply of food!

Perhaps the biggest threat facing our garden birds – indeed all Britain's birdlife – is global climate change. Once dismissed as mere fantasy, there is now no doubt that the coming century will see major climatic changes. These may result in Britain getting a warmer climate, though other scenarios are possible too. The main problem with climate change is that it alters habitat and food supply, and may also mean that breeding birds become out of synch with their insect prey, and as a result their young starve. Migrants may also be badly affected by drought in sub-Saharan Africa, where many species spend the winter.

It is hard to imagine, as we watch a House Martin or listen to a Blackbird singing, that these birds could potentially disappear from our towns and gardens. But this is not so far fetched as it might first appear. At least by providing food, water and nest sites for your garden birds, and by deterring pests and predators as best you can, you are giving the birds a vital helping hand in what may turn out to be a very difficult period in their lives.

Song Thrush

WATCHING BIRDS IN TOWNS

Once you have got to know the birds that regularly visit your garden, you may wish to venture farther afield. As a first step, a good move is to visit your local park. Parks vary a lot from place to place, but many provide a good range of habitats, including open grassy areas which attract thrushes (and early in the morning, Green Woodpeckers); small wooded areas which are good for warblers and other woodland species; and ideally an area of open water such as a lake, pond or stream.

Water always attracts a wide variety of birds, including the obvious ducks, geese and swans; coots and moorhens; and possibly rarer visitors such as grebes. In addition, many songbirds are attracted to water as a place to drink and bathe, so may also be seen here.

If you feel a bit more adventurous, then many other urban or suburban habitats can be good for birds. Walking along a river, even in the heart of a town or city, will often reveal some unexpected birds such as grebes, or if you are very lucky, a Kingfisher. Other 'wildlife corridors' include canals, railway embankments and scrubby bits of wood, all of which will act as communication routes and havens for all kinds of birds.

It is also worth looking on your local A to Z or Ordnance Survey map for areas without roads; or man-made habitats such as gravel pits. Another way to find out where to look for birds locally is to join your local bird club or get hold of a bird report covering your local area (usually county by county). Your local library should have the details of these.

Once you've found a good spot, consider visiting it regularly. A 'local patch' – a defined area with a variety of habitats which you can visit every week or so – will

Herring Gull

Robin

provide you with endless enjoyment, and an opportunity to get to know your local birds thoroughly. I've been going to a disused reservoir (now a local nature reserve) for a year or so now, and have already seen almost 100 different kinds of bird there!

If you are planning to venture a little farther afield, it's worth investing in a decent pair of binoculars to enable you to get good views, and to enjoy the experience. Check out the birding magazines for adverts from a specialist dealer near you, and don't be afraid to go along and ask for advice – that's what they are there for! Also you may find that you need a field guide – if so, choose something that gives good coverage to British birds. And don't forget your notebook – vital for when you are faced with a bird you can't identify.

Most of all, enjoy exploring your local area – and who knows, maybe one day you'll come across something really unusual. In the meantime, simply enjoy the pleasure you will get from watching common birds doing interesting things!

Golden Oriole

GREY HERON

Ardea cinerea

The largest bird ever likely to visit your garden, the Grey Heron is most often seen at dawn and dusk, as it makes a lightning raid to snatch fish from a garden pond. A shy bird, it may also be seen in flight overhead.

Identification A tall, statuesque bird, mainly grey in colour but with black on the head and wings, white on the face and neck, and a yellow, dagger-shaped bill. In flight looks huge, with hunched neck, broad wings and trailing legs.

Habits In gardens mainly comes to ponds, but elsewhere frequents rivers, streams and lakes, where it

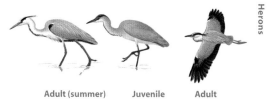

| Adult (summer) | Juvenile | Adult |

stands motionless, waiting patiently to strike at its aquatic prey. Herons are shy birds, and will usually fly when disturbed, though with patience you can get good views.

Feeding Mainly eats fish and other aquatic life such as frogs and newts, which it snatches using that powerful bill.

Breeding A colonial nester, breeding in 'heronries', usually at the tops of large trees, where it builds a nest from sticks. Breeds very early, laying in February or March. Lays 3–5 greenish-blue eggs, incubated for 25 days. Young fledge after 7–8 weeks. Usually one brood.

Voice A loud, deep and gruff croak, often uttered in flight.

When & where Resident. Widespread in suitable habitats throughout lowland Britain and Ireland. Currently increasing.

SPARROWHAWK

Accipter nisus

This specialised hunting machine has come back following a population crash in the 1960s, and is now our commonest garden bird predator. Despite its name, the Sparrowhawk hunts a variety of small birds, usually taken by surprise when feeding.

Identification A medium-sized, powerfully built raptor, with a long tail, rounded wings and hooked beak. Male smaller than female, with bluish back and rust-coloured underparts. Female browner, with heavy barring on chest. In flight can appear almost pigeon-shaped, though with stiffer wingbeats and more streamlined shape.

Habits Usually hunts by ambushing its prey from a bird feeder or the ground, grabbing it in its sharp talons before plucking its feathers with that powerful beak. Also soars high above gardens and parks, often flapping its wings followed by a short glide. However, can be shy so not always easily seen.

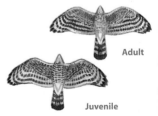

Adult

Juvenile

Feeding Feeds almost exclusively on small birds, especially finches, tits and sparrows; which it catches by seizing with its powerful claws.

Breeding Builds a large nest from twigs, usually in dense foliage of a mature tree. Lays 5–6 blotchy bluish-green and white eggs, incubated for 5 weeks. Young fledge after 3–4 weeks. One brood.

Voice A high-pitched, repetitive 'kew-kew-kew-kew-kew', mainly uttered during the breeding season.

When & where Resident. Found in well-wooded towns, villages and suburbs throughout lowland Britain and Ireland; often in gardens. Currently increasing after population crash in mid-20th century.

KESTREL

Falco tinnunculus

Britain's commonest bird of prey is a familiar sight as it hunts by hovering over roadsides, fields and verges. Originally a bird of the countryside, it has adapted well to living alongside human beings, often nesting on the roofs of buildings.

Identification Best identified in flight, by its slim, streamlined shape, with slender, pointed wings and long tail. Male smaller, with grey head, black moustaches and russet orange back. Female is bulkier, with streaked, not spotted back. In flight male shows dark wing tips contrasting with lighter back.

Habits Characteristic habit of hovering in one position, head motionless, in search of its rodent prey. Flies fast and direct, and occasionally soars on broader wings, when it may be mistaken for a Sparrowhawk.

Feeding Preys mainly on small rodents such as voles, though also takes small birds and even insects. Mostly hunts by hovering or by pouncing down from a perch.

Breeding Nests in tree holes and on roofs in towns and cities. Lays 3–6 pale eggs, blotched with reddish-brown, incubated for 4 weeks. Young fledge after 4–5 weeks. One brood.

Voice A far-carrying, high-pitched and repetitive 'kee-kee-kee', often uttered in flight.

When & where Resident. Found throughout Britain and Ireland apart from extreme north and west. Common in farmland habitats and along roadsides, especially motorway verges. Currently decreasing, especially in the countryside.

MOORHEN

Gallinula chloropus

Although a member of the rail family, the Moorhen, along with its close relative the Coot, is more like a duck in appearance. Although unobtrusive it is a widespread and familiar bird, especially on ponds in parks and villages.

Identification Superficially duck-like, but distinguished by its habit of bobbing while swimming, and the distinctive red-and-yellow bill. Adults are dark bluish-brown, with greyer flanks, a pale line of feathers

dividing upperparts and underparts, and a noticeable pale patch behind the cocked tail. Sexes similar.

Habits Often seen swimming along with its distinctive jaunty gait, or hiding shyly on the edge of reeds or aquatic vegetation. Also feeds on areas of wet grass, including lawns near streams or ponds. Unlike Coot, does not dive.

Feeding Feeds on a wide variety of underwater invertebrates, picked from off or just beneath the water surface, or from wet grass.

Breeding Builds a floating nest at the edge of a pond or lake. Lays an average of 7 eggs (often more), incubated for 3 weeks. Young fledge after 6–7 weeks, but can swim immediately after hatching. Two or three broods.

Voice A range of clucking calls, including a repetitive 'ki-ki-ki-kik'.

Adult

When & where Resident. Found on fresh water throughout lowland Britain and Ireland apart from the extreme north and west. Population currently stable.

Juvenile

BLACK-HEADED GULL

Larus ridibundus

Our most widespread gull, especially inland, where it has learned to live alongside human beings, scavenging for food on rubbish-tips and in cities. Most head away from urban areas to breed, returning in flocks for the autumn and winter.

Identification In spring and summer, its chocolate-brown hood makes it easy to identify from other, white-headed gulls. Outside the breeding season, identified by smaller size, pigeon-shaped appearance and dark spot behind ear. In flight pointed wings edged with white and tipped with black.

Habits A sociable bird, often gathering in flocks to feed, in open areas such as parks and playing fields. Squabbles over food, especially when raiding feeding stations in gardens. Roosts in huge flocks with other gulls on urban reservoirs, and often seen flying to and from feeding areas at dawn and dusk.

Feeding A catholic choice of food, including worms, bread and household food waste, scavenged from rubbish tips.

Breeding Breeds mainly in large colonies, often away from towns and cities. Lays 2–3 bluish-green eggs, blotched with brown and grey, incubated for 22–24 days. Young fledge after 5–6 weeks. One brood.

Voice A range of noisy calls, especially when in groups.

When & where Resident. Found throughout Britain and Ireland, though most obvious in autumn, winter and early spring, when large flocks come to towns and cities to feed and roost.

FERAL PIGEON

Columba livia

A largely despised and neglected bird, the Feral Pigeon originally descended from the wild Rock Dove, and was domesticated by our ancestors for food and sport. Today it has become a familiar, though not always welcome, sight in our towns and cities, where it lives happily alongside human beings.

Identification Feral Pigeons show a bewildering variety of different plumage features, with basic colours ranging from white, through browns and blacks, to the most typical grey of the wild ancestor. Many show two dark wing-bars and a white rump in flight.

Habits A highly sociable bird, almost always seen in flocks, sometimes numbering many hundreds of birds. Fascinating breeding behaviour, with males performing courtship display to females, especially in early spring and summer.

Feeding Can eat virtually anything even remotely edible – and occasionally pretty inedible! Can cause a hygiene problem if large numbers visit gardens to feed, so it is best not to encourage them.

Breeding Nests in holes and crevices, mainly in old buildings in urban and industrial areas. Lays 2 white eggs, incubated for 2–3 weeks. Young fledge after 4–5 weeks. Breeds almost all year round, with up to six broods. Fledged young resemble parents.

Voice A familiar, three noted cooing sound.

When & where Resident. Found throughout lowland Britain, especially in towns and cities, though much more localised in Scotland and Ireland. Population currently stable.

STOCK DOVE

Columba oenas

This often overlooked member of the pigeon family is found throughout much of Britain, and may be seen in parks and gardens, especially in rural and semi-rural areas. Look out for pairs displaying in early spring, or small groups of birds feeding in late summer.

Identification Slightly smaller and more delicate than the Wood Pigeon, with steel-grey plumage. Wings and tail tipped with black. Delicate yellow bill with red base, and greenish sheen on neck, distinctive. In flight appears 'squarer-winged' than other pigeons, and lacks white on wing.

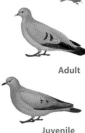

Habits Can be shy, sitting quietly in trees, so easy to miss. Will also feed in open areas, sometimes in flocks with other pigeon species, where identification made easier by direct comparison. In spring pairs undertake distinctive display flight from tops of large trees.

Adult

Juvenile

Feeding Mainly eats seeds, taken from the ground.

Adult

Breeding Stock Doves breed from late winter to late autumn, nesting in holes in trees, and laying 2 white eggs, incubated for 16–18 days. The young fledge after 3–4 weeks. A prolific breeder, which may have up to five broods.

Voice A soft pair of notes, repeated several times. Less raucous than its relatives.

When & where Resident. Found throughout lowland England, Wales and the south of Scotland, and in the south and east of Ireland. Generally increasing after earlier decline in middle of last century.

WOOD PIGEON

Columba palumbus

Adult

Although originally a bird of the open countryside, Wood Pigeons have rapidly adapted to life in towns and cities, and are now as familiar a sight in town parks and squares as their feral relative. A common visitor to gardens, where they feed readily on bird tables or the lawn.

Identification Our largest and bulkiest pigeon, easily identified by its distinctive white patch on the neck, and in flight, by the white stripes on its wings. Pale grey upperparts and a reddish-purple breast. Young lack white patch on neck.

Habits Although Wood Pigeons readily visit gardens and are found in most towns and cities, they can be shy and nervous, flying away as soon as they are disturbed.

Feeding Natural food includes seeds, berries and shoots, but urban pigeons will take a variety of other foods provided by humans. Often feeds beneath bird tables and feeders, picking up spilt seed from the ground.

Breeding Like other pigeons, breeds throughout the year, building a messy nest from twigs in a tree or bush. Lays 2 white eggs, incubated for 16–17 days. Young fledge after 3–5 weeks. Usually two broods.

Adult

Voice A distinctive, monotonous, five-note call: 'coo-COO-coo, coo-coo' – with the stress on the second syllable. One of the most familiar sounds of our towns and suburbs.

When & where Resident. Found throughout Britain and Ireland apart from the extreme uplands. Currently thriving, with numbers increasing rapidly.

COLLARED DOVE *Streptopelia decaocto*

Incredibly, this familiar and attractive little dove was not even a member of the British avifauna until the mid 1950s, when it first colonised following a rapid spread across Europe from western Asia. Now one of the most familiar birds of our towns, villages and suburban gardens.

Identification Easily told apart from other doves and pigeons by its pale, pinkish-brown plumage and the distinctive dark collar which gives the species its name. Dark wingtips, dark under the tail, and white outer tail-feathers, often noticeable in flight.

Habits In suburban areas often sits on roofs or fences, or visits bird tables and garden lawns in search of food. Spends much of its time in pairs or small groups.

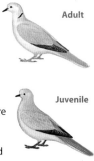

Adult

Juvenile

Feeding Like other pigeons and doves, has a marked preference for seeds. Can therefore be attracted by providing good quality seeds such as sunflower hearts, on a bird table or scattered on the ground.

Breeding Can nest all year round, though usually from February to October. Builds nest from sticks in thick foliage, and lays 2 white eggs, incubated for 14–18 days. Young fledge after 2–3 weeks. Several broods.

Adult

Voice A distinctive, though rather monotonous, three-noted call, 'coo-COO-coo', with the stress on the middle syllable.

When & where Resident. Found throughout lowland Britain, and more thinly distributed in Ireland. Prefers towns and suburbs, so absent from city centres. Currently increasing.

RING-NECKED PARAKEET
Psittacula krameri

Originally introduced by accident in the early 1970s, this brightly-coloured Asian parakeet has established a firm foothold in the London suburbs, where it thrives in parks and gardens. The jury is out on whether or not it will have a detrimental effect on our native birds, by taking over nest sites.

Identification Unmistakable: the only bright green bird in Britain, apart from the occasional escape from an aviary! Long and slender, with thin, pointed wings and a hooked bill. Adults have dark ring round collar, edged with pink on males.

Habits A noisy, sociable bird, often seen in large flocks. Will visit gardens to feed.

Feeding Eats a variety of fruits, berries and seeds, and has a marked preference for monkey nuts in their shells, which it breaks open to get at the peanuts inside.

Breeding Nests in holes in trees, laying 2–4 white eggs, incubated for 22–24 days. Young fledge after 6–7 weeks. One, sometimes two, broods.

Voice A loud, high-pitched screech, usually uttered as a contact call in flight. Can also utter a repeated call reminiscent of that of the Green Woodpecker.

When & where Common but very locally distributed in parts of south-east England, including the west London suburbs around the River Thames and Richmond Park, and also in parts of Kent and Sussex. Best observed at dusk as they fly into their communal roosts.

Adult male

Adult female

TAWNY OWL

Strix aluco

Our commonest and most widespread owl, yet paradoxically one of the hardest of its family to see, due to its nocturnal lifestyle. Your best chance of seeing one is at a winter roost, where a bird will often sit in a visible position in a hole of a tree.

Identification Best identified by its distinctive calls: the famous hooting, and a loud, high-pitched 'kee-

Adult

Adult

wick'. If seen, a classic 'owl shape': dark brown with round face and medium build. Rarely seen in flight, on rounded wings and with stealthy appearance.

Habits Virtually exclusively nocturnal, though may sometimes be seen at daytime roost, especially in autumn and winter. Highly sedentary, rarely venturing more than a mile from its home territory.

Feeding Feeds mainly on rodents, especially rats, mice and voles, but will also take birds and amphibians, especially during harsh winter weather. Hunts with great effect on silent wings, pouncing on its unsuspecting prey.

Breeding Nests in hole in tree, laying between 2 and 5 round white eggs, incubated for about 4 weeks. Young fledge after 5 weeks, though often leave nest beforehand, and may be visible nearby. One brood.

Voice Distinctive, haunting, hooting call, and piercing 'kee-wick', with stress on second note.

When & where Resident. Found throughout wooded areas of Britain, including towns and suburbs, but absent from north and west Scotland and not found at all in Ireland. Currently decreasing.

SWIFT

Apus apus

The ultimate flying machine, the Swift is one of the best-known summer visitors to our towns and cities. Arriving in late April or early May, Swifts announce their arrival by flying through the city skyscape, screaming as they go.

Adults

Identification
Although superficially similar to Swallows and Martins, the Swift is in fact highly distinctive, with its all dark plumage, cigar shaped body and narrow, swept back wings. A closer look reveals that the plumage is in fact dark brown, not black as it may first appear.

Habits Spends its entire time (apart from when at the nest) in flight, sweeping across the sky singly or in sociable groups. At night flies high into the sky in search of insects, and to snatch brief moments of sleep.

Juvenile

Feeding Feeds entirely on small flying insects, caught on the wing. Snatches them from the air using its huge gape.

Breeding Nests in roofs of buildings, laying 2–3 white eggs, incubated for between 3–4 weeks. The young fledge after 5–8 weeks, depending on the weather and resulting food availability. One brood.

Voice Distinctive screaming, which in the past earned them the nickname of 'devil bird'. Most obvious at dusk.

When & where Summer visitor, from late April to July or August. Found in towns, villages and cities throughout Britain and Ireland, apart from extreme north and west. Currently in rapid decline, possibly because of lack of nest sites.

KINGFISHER

Alcedo atthis

Britain's most colourful, and arguably most beautiful, bird is a scarce but regular visitor to gardens, especially those near water. It can also be found along streams and by lakes, even near the centre of towns and cities.

Identification Absolutely unmistakable! Dazzling electric blue upperparts and deep orange underparts make it stand out like a sore thumb! Often seen darting away in flight, when often looks smaller than

expected. If seen perched look out for the orange on the base of the bill – females have it, males don't.

Habits Shy and retiring, it often sits perched quietly and only flies at the last moment, dashing away up the stream or river. Hunts by pouncing down from a perch, plunging beneath the water to catch tiny fish.

Feeding Almost exclusively feeds on fish and small aquatic invertebrates, taken from on or beneath the water surface.

Adult female

Breeding Nests deep in a hole in a bank of a river, lake or stream. Lays 5–7 white eggs, incubated for 19–20 days. Young fledge after 3–4 weeks, and will continue to be fed outside the nest. Two, occasionally three, broods.

Voice A high-pitched whistling call.

When & where Resident, though may move to the coast during the winter. Found in suitable habitats – near rivers, lakes or streams – throughout lowland England and Wales; scarce in Ireland and Scotland. Occasional visitor to gardens. Currently increasing.

GREEN WOODPECKER   *Picus viridis*

The largest of our three species of woodpecker, and much bigger than its two 'spotted' relatives. Usually seen feeding on lawns or in long grass, and although shy, may allow close approach before it flies away. Also may be seen climbing trees, where it occasionally drums to attract a mate.

Identification With its yellow-green plumage, bright red cap and black face mask, this woodpecker is easy to identify. Young birds lack the black on face. In flight watch out for heavy, pot-bellied shape and undulating motion.

Habits Unlike other woodpeckers, spends much of its time on the ground, where it feeds on ants. Likes large gardens with spacious lawns, often visiting at dawn or dusk to avoid disturbance.

Feeding Mainly on ants, which it sweeps up from the ground using a specially adapted sticky tongue.

Breeding Nests in a hole in a tree which it excavates itself in early spring. Lays 5–7 white eggs, incubated for 17–19 days. Young fledge after 18–21 days. One brood.

Voice A loud, powerful series of high-pitched notes,

reminiscent of a laughing sound, and giving the species the country name of 'Yaffle'. Said to call more just before rain!

When & where
Resident. Found in suitable habitat (mixed woodland, parks and large gardens) throughout England, Wales and southern Scotland. Like all woodpeckers, absent from Ireland. Currently stable or increasing.

Adult

Juvenile

GREAT SPOTTED WOODPECKER

Dendrocopos major

The largest of the two 'spotted' woodpeckers, and by far the most numerous and widespread – any black and white woodpecker you see is almost certain to be this species. Frequently visits gardens, especially during autumn and winter, even feeding on bird tables and peanut feeders.

Identification Roughly size of Starling, with obvious contrasting black and white plumage, notably two large oval patches on back. Males have red on back of head; females lack this. Juveniles have completely red cap. In flight has undulating action.

Habits The classic woodpecker in behaviour and habits: often seen climbing up and around a branch or tree trunk, searching for insect food, or flying from tree to tree. An excellent climber, using specially adapted feet and tail.

Feeding Feeds mainly on insects and grubs, prised from the surface or beneath the bark of a tree. Will also feed on peanuts from feeders, and raid nest holes and nestboxes to get baby birds.

Breeding Nests in specially excavated hole in tree,

laying 4–7 white eggs, incubated for 16 days. Young fledge after 18–24 days. One brood.

Voice Loud, far carrying drumming in spring; also distinctive, resonant 'chip' call, which often draws your attention to its presence high in a tree.

When & where Resident. Found throughout England, Wales and most of lowland Scotland, but completely absent from Ireland. Currently increasing rapidly.

Adult female

Juvenile

LESSER SPOTTED WOODPECKER

Dendrocopos minor

Our smallest woodpecker, and by far the scarcest of the three British species. Its shy and furtive habits also make it by far the hardest to see. Does visit large, mature gardens, but often only given away by its call or a quiet, soft drumming sound.

Identification If seen well, told apart from its larger Great Spotted relative by its much smaller size, barred black and white back (not oval patches), and small bill. Male has red patch on forehead, while female has white crown.

Adult female

Habits In behaviour, more like a Nuthatch or Treecreeper than other members of its family. Most likely to be seen climbing around

Juvenile

the trunk or branch of a mature tree. In winter also joins tit flocks, where it may easily be overlooked.

Feeding Creeps around the trunks and branches of trees searching for small, wood boring insects and grubs, which it digs out using its sharp bill. Rarely visits bird feeding stations.

Breeding Nests in specially excavated hole in branch of tree, often very high up. Lays 4–6 white eggs, incubated for 11–14 days. Young fledge after 18–21 days. One brood.

Voice Quiet, gentle drumming. High-pitched, repetitive call – a weak 'kee-kee-kee-kee'.

When & where Resident. Found in mature woodland all over southern Britain, though very scarce in Scotland and absent from Ireland. Currently undergoing major decline in numbers.

SWALLOW

Hirundo rustica

Surely our most familiar and welcome summer visitor, the Swallow makes the epic 5,000 mile journey to and from southern Africa each spring and autumn. Once here, it is a familiar sight in most rural areas, often living alongside people in farms and villages.

Adult male

Identification A slim, elegant bird, with a longer tail than the martins or Swift. Dark blue above, cream below, with a reddish throat. Usually seen in flight, where its elegant shape and low flying habits make it one of the most delightful birds to watch.

Juvenile

Habits Flies low over fields, open grassy areas or water, hunting for small flying insects. Especially in later summer and early autumn, look out for them on telegraph wires, as they prepare for the long journey south.

Feeding Feeds almost entirely on small insects, caught in its acrobatic flight.

Breeding Usually nests in old buildings, especially barns and old houses. Builds a cup-shaped nest from mud, and lays 4–5 white eggs with reddish brown spotting, incubated for 14–16 days. Young fledge after 3 weeks. Two, sometimes three, broods.

Voice Series of chattering notes, usually given in flight. Also a high-pitched 'chit'.

When & where Summer visitor, arriving in early April and departing in September or October. Found throughout lowland Britain and Ireland, even in the far north, though absent from big cities. Currently in decline.

HOUSE MARTIN   *Delichon urbica*

One of the classic birds of urban and suburban Britain, the House Martin is a familiar sight throughout spring and summer, as flocks fly over our villages, towns and cities, giving their characteristic twittering calls. Depends on humans for nesting sites, as its name suggests!

Identification Given good views, easily told apart from Swallow and Swift by its smaller size, more compact shape, shallowly forked tail, and white rump. Upperparts dark bluish-black; underparts white. Closely related Sand Martin much browner, and lacks the House Martin's white rump.

Habits Generally seen in flight, hawking for insect food over houses. Like Swallows, House Martins gather on telegraph wires in late summer and autumn, in preparation for migration south to Africa.

Adult

Feeding Feeds almost entirely on small flying insects, caught on the wing.

Breeding Builds characteristic nest out of tiny balls of mud, usually under the eaves of houses. Will also use artificial nestboxes. Lays 3–5 whitish eggs, incubated for 14–16 days. Young fledge after 2–3 weeks. Two, sometimes three, broods.

Voice A rapid series of high-pitched, twittering sounds; also a sharp, loud 'prrrit' call.

When & where Summer visitor, arriving mid-April and departing in September. Found throughout lowland Britain and Ireland, apart from extreme north and west. Currently declining, possibly as a result of shortage of mud to build nests, though also because of drought in their African winter quarters.

GREY WAGTAIL

Motacilla cinerea

This elegant bird surely deserves a better name – perhaps 'lemon-bellied' – to reflect its colourful appearance. At home on streams and rivers, it may also be seen in gardens and parks, especially near water.

Identification More elegant and slimmer in appearance than the commoner Pied Wagtail, with steel grey upperparts and lemon-yellow underparts. Told from similar Yellow Wagtail (a summer visitor) by shape and colour pattern. In breeding season males have black throat, which in winter turns white. In flight appears very long and slim, with bounding flight action.

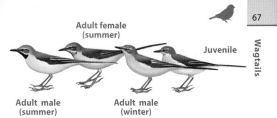

Adult female (summer)

Juvenile

Adult male (summer)

Adult male (winter)

Habits Like all wagtails has characteristic gait, wagging tail up and down as it walks. Usually seen by or very near water, hunting for food amongst the shallows or on stones or rocks. Flies low over water, often calling.

Feeding Feeds almost entirely on insects, but will also take tiny aquatic invertebrates and small fish.

Breeding Nests very near a river or stream, usually building a nest in a hole, crack or crevice inside a wall or stone bridge. Lays 4–6 buff, spotted eggs, incubated for 11–14 days. Two, sometimes three, broods.

Voice A loud, piercing two-note call, similar to Pied Wagtail's, but sharper and more metallic in sound.

When & where Resident. Found in suitable habitat throughout lowland Britain and Ireland, though rare or absent from parts of eastern England. Currently on the increase.

PIED WAGTAIL

Motacilla alba

Our commonest and most familiar wagtail, and a regular and frequent visitor to towns, parks and gardens. Can often be seen searching for food along a pavement or a grassy verge, and is equally at home feeding on open lawns.

Identification The only long tailed, small, black and white bird in the region. Basically black and grey above and white below, with a black throat. Females appear greyer, while juveniles can look very brown in colour. In flight long tail and bounding flight very distinctive.

Habits Usually seen walking back and forth across pavement or grass while looking for tiny morsels of food. Will also perch on roofs. Very sociable, especially in winter, when several dozen may gather to roost for warmth.

Feeding Feeds mainly on tiny insects and other invertebrates, picked up in its sharp, pointed bill.

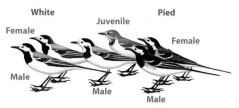

White   Juvenile   Pied

Female

Male   Male   Female

Male

Breeding Nests in holes in walls, building a small nest lined with hair and feathers. Lays 5–6 pale eggs finely spotted darker, incubated for 11–16 days. Young fledge after just 11–16 days, making it one of the shortest periods between laying and fledging. Two or three broods.

Voice A loud, distinctive two note call, usually written 'chis-ick', with the emphasis on the second syllable.

When & where Resident. Found throughout Britain and Ireland, apart from extreme uplands. Common in our cities. Population currently stable.

WAXWING
Bombycilla garrulus

One of our rarest and most distinctive town and garden birds, the Waxwing is in fact an irregular visitor, whose arrival in autumn is governed by food supplies in its sub-Arctic home. Some years see many thousands of birds; other years virtually none. Arrivals spend the winter around berry bushes before returning north in spring.

Identification Given good views, hard to confuse with any other bird. Starling sized: plump, with soft brown plumage, a distinctive crest, and red and yellow markings on wings that give the species its name.

Adult

Habits Very sociable, usually seen in flocks of up to several dozen birds. These often arrive, strip a berry bush bare, and depart within a day or two in search of more food.

Feeding In winter, prefers berries, especially red ones such as cotoneaster, which the birds will strip from a tree or bush. May also 'flycatch' for small insects, especially in mild, sunny weather.

Juvenile

Breeding Does not breed in Britain or Ireland. Home range is in sub-Arctic Scandinavia and Russia.

Voice A quiet, delicate trilling call, often uttered by several birds at once.

When & where Autumn and winter visitor, usually arriving in October or November and departing back to Scandinavia and Russia in March or April. May be seen almost anywhere, but commonest in coastal eastern counties of England and Scotland. During 'irruption years' there may be many thousands of Waxwings in the country.

WREN

Troglodytes troglodytes

Our commonest breeding bird, the Wren is not as well known as some other species because of its skulking habits and small size. Yet it lives in most gardens, being able to adapt to a wide variety of habitats.

Identification The only small bird which habitually cocks its tail. Tiny, russet brown above, paler buffish brown below, with barring on the flanks and a short pale stripe behind the eye. Most often heard before it is seen – its trilling song is one of the loudest of any songbird.

Habits Often skulks around, hopping about in a rockery or base of a shrubbery in search of tiny morsels of food. Rarely seen in flight – tiny whirring wings distinctive.

Adult

Feeding Feeds on small insects and other invertebrates, found by foraging in soil, or in the spaces between rocks or stones.

Breeding Builds a hidden, dome-shaped nest, often in a

Juvenile

garden. Lays 5–8 whitish eggs, incubated for 12–20 days. Young fledge after 2–3 weeks. Two broods.

Voice Extraordinarily loud and piercing song: full of trills and ending with a rapid series of notes. Call a loud 'tic'.

When & where Resident. Found throughout Britain and Ireland, in almost all habitats including rocky islands and sea-cliffs as well as parks and gardens. Extraordinarily resilient and adaptable for such a small bird. Currently increasing thanks to very mild winters.

DUNNOCK

Prunella modularis

Often overlooked or mistaken for a female House Sparrow, the Dunnock is one of our commonest and most fascinating garden birds, with an amazing sex life! Once known as the 'hedge sparrow', in fact it is a member of the accentor family.

Identification Superficially sparrow-like, though its shape more like that of a Robin. On closer look the purplish grey head, face and throat, contrasting with a reddish brown back, are distinctive. Posture also more horizontal, like a Robin. Juveniles are streakier below, and less colourful.

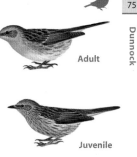

Habits A shy, retiring bird, often found deep in a shrubbery or at the edge of a flower-bed. In the breeding season males become more active and can be seen chasing each other around the garden, as they pursue several females at once.

Adult

Juvenile

Feeding Feeds mainly on small insects and other invertebrates, picked up from the ground, though will also take seeds, especially in winter.

Breeding Builds a cup-shaped nest in dense foliage, from twigs and grass lined with hair and feathers. Lays 4–6 sky blue eggs, incubated for 12–13 days. Young fledge after 11–12 days. Two, sometimes three, broods. Males breed with several females.

Voice Rather monotonous song; a soft warble with no clear beginning or end.

When & where Resident. Found throughout Britain and Ireland apart from the extreme north and west. Currently declining.

ROBIN

Erithacus rubecula

Britain's favourite garden bird is also one of our most familiar: loved by gardeners for its confiding habits. Originally a woodland species, the Robin has adapted well to living alongside human beings, and is welcome in any garden. To attract them, try digging your flower beds or bribing them with tasty mealworms!

Identification An adult Robin, with its orange-red breast and throat, brown upperparts bordered with grey, and black beady eye, is unmistakable. Juvenile is same shape as adult but has speckled plumage for camouflage after leaving the nest.

Adult

Juvenile

Habits Generally seen hopping about on the lawn, on rockeries, or in undergrowth, where it searches for insect food. Will also come to bird tables, and seed and nut feeders. Some birds will even feed from the hand.

Feeding Generally insectivorous, but also feeds on seeds, especially in winter. Loves mealworms!

Breeding An early breeder, building a cup-shaped nest in a shrub or bush, or sometimes in unusual sites such as lavatory cisterns. Will use open-fronted nestboxes. Lays 5–7 bluish-white eggs, incubated for 12–14 days. Young fledge after 12–15 days. Two, sometimes three, broods.

Voice Beautiful, plaintive song; sung in sweet phrases. Robins sing all year round as they defend autumn and winter territories. Variety of calls including sharp 'tic'.

When & where Resident, with immigrants from Europe in autumn and winter. Found throughout Britain and Ireland. Common and currently thriving.

BLACKBIRD

Turdus merula

One of our most familiar birds, the Blackbird is in fact a member of the thrush family. Originally a woodland species, it has adapted very well to nesting and feeding in towns and gardens. Famed for its glorious song.

Identification Male lives up to his name: black plumage with a yellow bill. Female is mid brown in colour, with some pale streaking on throat and breast. Juveniles speckly, and can be mistaken for a Song or Mistle Thrush at first sight, though lack the clear breast markings.

Habits A confident bird, often feeding in the open on lawns, where it pulls up worms with that powerful beak. Territorially aggressive, with males chasing each other off, especially during the spring.

Feeding Feeds mainly on earthworms and other invertebrates, dug up from lawns and flower beds. In autumn and winter will also feed on windfall apples and berries.

Adult female

First winter male

Juvenile

Adult male

Breeding Builds neat, cup-shaped nest of grasses lined with mud, usually in a bush or shrub. Lays 3–5 greenish eggs spotted with reddish brown, incubated for 12–15 days. Young fledge after 12–15 days. Up to five broods in a single season.

Voice Distinctive, tuneful song, with rich tone and clear phrases. Variety of calls, such as the chattering alarm when flushed.

When & where Resident. Found throughout Britain and Ireland, apart from highland areas. Common, but recently undergone decline.

FIELDFARE

Turdus pilaris

This large thrush is a winter visitor to our shores, arriving in autumn and staying until spring, before it heads north and east to breed. Usually found on farmland, often in the company of other thrushes such as the Redwing.

Identification Almost as big as a Mistle Thrush, and superficially similar, but much more colourful, with yellow bill, grey head, russet upperparts and pale yellow underparts streaked with black. In undulating flight appears pot bellied and bulky, with grey rump contrasting with darker tail and wings.

Habits A noisy, sociable bird, which often forms large flocks to feed, either perching in bushes or on the ground. Like other thrushes will sometimes defend a particular bush against intruders.

Feeding Feeds mainly on fruit and berries, taken either from the bush or as windfall from the ground.

Breeding Breeds mainly in Scandinavia, eastern Europe and Russia, though a few pairs breed annually in northern and eastern Britain, especially Scotland.

Voice A loud, harsh and repetitive 'chack' call, often given in flight.

When & where An autumn and winter visitor to most areas of Britain and Ireland, though commoner in the milder south and east of the country. Not as common in towns as other members of its family, but will visit gardens during harsh winter weather. Numbers vary from year to year, depending on breeding success in home range.

Adult

Juvenile

SONG THRUSH   *Turdus philomelos*

One of our best loved garden birds, the Song Thrush has recently suffered a huge and sudden population decline, probably due to lack of food caused by modern farming methods. What was once the classic 'sound of the suburbs' has now fallen silent in some areas, though it is still found in many parks and gardens.

Identification A small, neat thrush, with the classic brown back, and pale underparts spotted with blackish brown. Song also very distinctive: a repeated series of phrases, usually in groups of three.

Adult

Habits In early spring, perches on a roof or tree to herald the new season with its lovely song. Otherwise often unobtrusive as it forages for food in shrubberies, flower beds and on lawns.

Juvenile

Feeding Feeds mainly on earthworms, slugs and snails, so very popular amongst gardeners as a means of natural pest control!

Breeding Builds a neat, cup-shaped nest lined with mud, in a bush or shrub. Lays 3–5 sky blue eggs speckled with tiny black spots, incubated for 12–14 days. Young fledge after 12–15 days. Two, sometimes three, broods.

Voice Rich, tuneful and melodic song, with clear groups of phrases, usually in threes.

When & where Resident, though some immigrants from Europe in winter. Found throughout Britain and Ireland, apart from upland areas of Scotland. Relies heavily on gardens for places to nest and feed. Currently in severe decline.

REDWING

Turdus iliacus

Our smallest thrush is primarily an autumn and winter visitor to Britain and Ireland, though a few pairs do stay to breed, virtually all in northern Scotland. Like its larger cousin the Fieldfare, the Redwing often gathers in flocks to seek out food.

Identification Slightly smaller than Song Thrush, and much darker in overall appearance. Surprisingly, the orangey red patch on the flanks that gives the species its name is not always the first thing you notice – the creamy eye-stripe is often a better identification feature.

Habits A sociable bird, generally seen in small groups or larger flocks, along with other members of its family. Will frequently come to gardens to feed, especially those near open fields. Most likely to be seen during harsh winter weather, when food is scarce.

Feeding Feeds mainly on berries, either taken direct from a bush or from the ground. Like other thrushes, is also partial to windfall fruit, especially apples.

Breeding A rare breeder in Britain, and unlikely to do so in gardens or towns.

Voice A thin, high-pitched call, generally given in flight. Listen out for migrating redwings during clear autumn nights as they pass overhead, often in quite large flocks.

Adult

When & where Autumn and winter visitor, arriving in October and November and departing northwards to breed in March or April. Common and widespread throughout Britain and Ireland.

Juvenile

MISTLE THRUSH

Turdus viscivorus

Adult

Our largest thrush, almost the size and bulk of a pigeon, the Mistle Thrush is named for its love of the berries of the Mistletoe, though like other members of its family it is partial to all berries and fruits.

Identification Much larger and noticeably paler in appearance than Song Thrush, with greyish brown upperparts, and pale underparts thickly spotted with black. In flight, pale underwings and large size obvious. Told apart from similar sized Fieldfare by lack of colour on head, back and underparts.

Juvenile

Habits In summer, males often sit high on a prominent tree, delivering their characteristic song. In autumn and winter travels in large flocks, often chattering as they fly overhead. Will also defend berry bushes against all comers.

Feeding In spring and summer feeds mainly on earthworms and other invertebrates, taken from the soil or ground. In autumn and winter prefers fruit and berries.

Breeding Builds a large nest, usually in the fork of a mature tree, and lays 3–5 greenish-blue eggs, with light brown speckling, which are incubated for 12–15 days. Young fledge after 12–16 days. Two, occasionally three, broods.

Voice Song like a cross between a Song Thrush and Blackbird, with the repetition of the former and rich tone of the latter. Harsh rattling call, usually given in flight.

When & where Resident. Common and widespread in suitable habitat – parks and large gardens – throughout Britain and Ireland. Currently decreasing rapidly.

WHITETHROAT

Sylvia communis

Though often overlooked, this is in fact one of our commonest and most widespread summer visitors, widely found in suitable scrubby habitat. Over 30 years ago the species suffered a major population crash due to drought in Africa, but it has since bounced back and is currently doing well.

Identification A slender, brightly coloured warbler. Males have a chestnut brown back and wings, grey head and prominent white throat, which is puffed out when singing. Female duller than male. In flight appears very slim and long tailed.

Adult male

Adult female

Juvenile

Habits A fairly skulking bird, though singing males will sit up on a bush or launch themselves into the air on a parachuting song flight! Best searched for on calm, sunny days in May.

Feeding Feeds mainly on small insects, caught in flight or taken from vegetation.

Breeding Builds cup-shaped nest, hidden low in bushes such as brambles, and lays 4–5 buffish white eggs with darker spots, incubated for 11–13 days. Young fledge after 10–12 days. One, often two, broods.

Voice A variety of vocalisations, including a fast, chattering warble and several harsh calls.

When & where Summer visitor, arriving in April and leaving in September for its winter quarters in sub-Saharan Africa. Common and widespread in suitable habitat throughout England and Wales; more thinly spread in Scotland and Ireland, and absent from the far north. Currently on the increase, but highly vulnerable to drought in Africa.

GARDEN WARBLER

Sylvia borin

One of our least known and most unobtrusive songbirds, this widespread species is easily overlooked. Despite its name it is not a common visitor to gardens, and is best looked for in mature woodland with open canopies.

Identification A large warbler, greyish brown in overall appearance, and with few obvious identification features. Most similar to Blackcap in shape, but lacks black or brown cap, and plumage more olive coloured in tone. Plain face and beady eye, with faint eye-stripe. Thick, greyish bill and dark legs.

Habits Shy and elusive, often skulking in low vegetation, though singing males may sit in a more prominent and visible position.

Feeding Feeds mainly on tiny insects, which it obtains by 'gleaning' – picking them off leaves and other foliage with its bill.

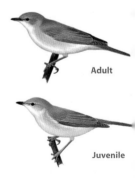

Adult

Juvenile

Breeding Builds a cup-shaped nest in thick foliage, usually near to the ground, and lays 4–5 pale eggs with fine brown spots, incubated for 10–12 days. Young fledge after only 9–12 days. One, sometimes two, broods.

Voice Song very easily confused with that of the Blackcap, its close relative. With practice, can be told apart by faster pace and less fluty tone.

When & where Summer visitor, arriving in early to mid-May, and leaving in August or early September. Reasonably widespread but thinly distributed throughout lowland England and Wales; less common in southern Scotland, and a few pairs in Ireland.

BLACKCAP

Sylvia atricapilla

One of our commonest and most widespread warblers, this species was once exclusively a summer visitor to Britain, but in recent years birds from continental Europe have begun to spend the whole of the winter here, often visiting gardens to feed on berries and fruit.

Adult male (summer)

Identification If seen well, fairly easy to identify: a large, fairly bulky, grey warbler with a black cap (male) or chestnut-brown one (female). Beware confusion

with Marsh Tit, which is superficially similar in appearance but has a very different shape and habits.

Habits In spring and summer best sought out by listening for its distinctive fluty song. In autumn and winter more likely to visit gardens, either feeding on berries or coming to feeders.

Feeding In summer feeds mainly on insects, but in autumn and winter has a more varied diet including berries. Very partial to hanging 'fat bars'.

Juvenile

Breeding Builds nest in low, thick bushes or shrubs, laying 4–6 pale eggs with fine brown spots, incubated for 10–12 days. Young fledge after 10–13 days. One or two broods.

Voice Distinctive, fluty song, reminiscent of Blackbird in tone but at a higher pitch. Call a hard 'tac'.

When & where Summer visitors arrive in March or April and depart in September or October. Winter visitors overlap, arriving in autumn and departing in the spring. Common and widespread throughout Britain apart from northern Scotland; scarce in Ireland.

CHIFFCHAFF
Phylloscopus collybita

One of our commonest and most familiar warblers, this tiny bird usually announces its arrival in spring with the familiar song which gives the species its name. In recent years Chiffchaffs have also begun to spend the winter in southern and western Britain.

Identification Very similar to Willow Warbler, though more olive and brown in tone, and with a less prominent eye-stripe and dark legs. Best identified by its famous song, which can be heard from early in the spring season, before most other migrants have returned.

Habits Most easily observed when feeding or singing, as it flits around the canopy of trees. Often delivers its song sitting out on a prominent perch.

Adult (spring)

Feeding Feeds mainly on insects, though wintering birds have adapted to taking seeds from bird tables and artificial feeders.

Juvenile

Breeding Builds its nest hidden very low in dense vegetation or on the ground, and lays 4–7 pale eggs with dark spots, incubated for 13–15 days. Young fledge after 12–15 days. One, sometimes two, broods.

Voice The famous repeated phrase of two notes: 'chiff' and 'chaff'! Also distinctive 'hoo-eeet' call.

When & where During the breeding season common and widespread throughout England, Wales and most of Ireland; less widely distributed in Scotland. Wintering birds found mostly in southern and western England, Wales and Ireland, where the milder climate enables them to find food. Currently on the increase.

GOLDCREST

Regulus regulus

Europe's smallest bird, the Goldcrest is closely related to the leaf warblers such as Willow Warbler and Chiffchaff, which it superficially resembles. Despite its tiny size the Goldcrest is well able to survive very harsh winter weather, retreating deep into forests to feed.

Identification Tiny, plump and compact (weighing just 5 grams), this little greenish coloured bird is best identified by its orange (male) or yellow (female) crown. Closer views reveal a black, beady eye, and pale wing bar. In flight appears short winged and short tailed.

Male

Habits Often hidden deep in foliage, where it gleans for tiny insects, hovering on whirring wings as it does so. Can be very confiding, especially in winter.

Feeding Feeds on tiny insects and other invertebrates, picked up using its thin bill.

Breeding Builds a very small nest, hanging off the end of a twig, often in a conifer tree or bush. Lays 7–12 tiny eggs, pale with fine buff spots, incubated for 16 days. Young fledge after 19 days. Two broods, often close together.

Voice Thin, high-pitched 'see-see-see' call often the first indication of its presence. Song a distinctive, high-pitched phrase, with a rapid rhythm on three repeated notes.

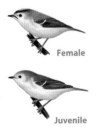

Female

Juvenile

When & where Resident, though immigrants from Scandinavia augment numbers in autumn and winter. Common and widespread throughout most of Britain and Ireland. Often visits gardens, especially outside the breeding season. Currently decreasing.

SPOTTED FLYCATCHER

Muscicapa striata

This delightful summer visitor is now sadly decreasing in numbers, possibly due to a lack of insect food, or perhaps because of drought on its African wintering grounds. Can still be seen flycatching for food in many rural areas, though.

Identification A slim, brownish bird, with a distinctive upright stance, beady eye and long, thin bill. Upperparts brown, darker on wings; underparts buff streaked with fine darker lines on throat and sides of breast. Best identified by its characteristic flycatching on long, slender wings.

Habits Habit of launching itself into the air to catch flying insects gives the species its name. Generally quite confiding, with a preference for sunny, walled gardens where it can build a nest and catch food.

Adult

Juvenile

Feeding Feeds exclusively on small flying insects caught on the wing or gleaned from leaves.

Breeding Builds a nest in a crevice or crack in a wall, and lays 4–6 buff or bluish eggs speckled with red, incubated for 12–14 days. Young fledge after 14 days or so. One, sometimes two broods, especially in warm, dry summers.

Voice Series of high pitched squeaky notes, delivered from a perch on a branch.

When & where Summer visitor, not arriving until mid May, and departing south again by September. Found throughout Britain and Ireland, though commonest in the south and east. Currently undergoing major decline, which may be difficult to reverse.

LONG-TAILED TIT   *Aegithalos caudatus*

This delightful little bird is one of our most distinctive: its long tail and fluffy body make it hard to confuse with any other species. A sociable bird, it usually travels in family parties, calling to one another as they go.

Identification Given good views, hard to mistake for any other species. Plumage a combination of dark brown, white, cream and pinkish-buff, though young birds are less colourful and have darker markings on the head and neck. Shape like a ball of fluff with a long tail!

Habits Usually heard before it is seen, then appears, stops momentarily to feed, before passing on with the remainder of its flock. Can be extremely confiding, especially in autumn and winter.

Feeding Feeds on tiny insects and also spiders, obtained by picking off leaves and bark with that tiny bill.

Breeding Builds an extraordinary, barrel-shaped nest out of feathers, spiders' webs and lichen, low in a bush such as a bramble. Lays 7–12 tiny white eggs, incubated for 13–17 days. Young fledge after 15–16 days, accompanying their parents for some time afterwards. One brood.

Voice Distinctive high-pitched contact call, repeated to keep in touch with other members of its flock.

Adult

When & where
Resident. Found throughout England, Wales and much of Scotland; scarcer and less widespread in Ireland. Often visits gardens, especially after the breeding season and during the autumn and winter. Currently increasing, thanks to mild winters.

Juvenile

MARSH TIT

Parus palustris

Although not as common or widespread as its commoner relatives, the Marsh Tit is nevertheless a fairly regular visitor to gardens, especially in rural areas of England and Wales. Can be confused with the very similar looking Willow Tit.

Identification A medium sized tit, mainly brown with paler underparts and a black cap and bib. Told from Willow Tit by less bulky appearance, glossy cap and lack of pale patch on wing. Told from Coal Tit by larger size and lack of white patch on back of neck.

Habits Like all tits, partial to feeding on seeds and peanuts, and will regularly come to bird tables and feeders, especially in gardens near woodland. Shyer and less dominant than Blue or Great Tits, often waiting its turn to feed.

Feeding Feeds mainly on insects during the breeding season, and nuts and seeds in autumn and winter.

Breeding Builds nest in a hole in a tree (or occasionally a nestbox), laying 7–11 white eggs spotted with red, incubated for 13–15 days. Young fledge after 17–21 days. One brood.

Adult   **Juvenile**

Voice Song a repeated phrase of notes rather like Blue Tit. Call an explosive 'pit-choo' – often the best indication of its presence.

When & where
Resident. Found in suitable wooded habitat and large gardens throughout England and Wales, with a very few breeding in southern Scotland. Completely absent from Ireland. Currently in decline.

COAL TIT

Parus ater

This neat little bird is usually found in or near coniferous woods and forests, though is adaptable enough to venture in to gardens in search of a free meal. Like all its family it performs acrobatic feats in order to obtain food, though usually defers to its commoner relatives in the feeding station pecking order.

Adult

Identification A small, active little bird, with a distinctive white patch on the nape (back of the neck), white cheeks and a black head and bib. Upperparts brown with white wingbar; underparts buffy-white.

Habits A sociable bird, often feeding with other tit species, especially during autumn and winter when they form mixed flocks. More fond of conifers than its relatives, and often seen in the company of Goldcrests.

Juvenile

Feeding Feeds on tiny insects during spring and summer, but from autumn onwards will visit gardens in search of seeds and nuts from feeders.

Breeding Builds a compact nest out of moss, often in a cavity in a branch or tree stump. Lays 8–9 white eggs spotted with reddish brown, incubated for 13–18 days. Young fledge after 16–22 days. One, sometimes two, broods.

Voice Rhythmic song rather like gentle version of Great Tit. Calls a series of thin, high-pitched squeaks, inaudible to some human ears.

When & where Resident. Found throughout suitable habitat in Britain and Ireland apart from the extreme north. Currently on the increase.

BLUE TIT

Parus caeruleus

Our commonest and most widespread species of tit, found in virtually every garden in the country. Amongst the first species of bird to adapt to artificial seed and peanut feeders, and has also learned to raid milk bottles in search of cream! Also readily takes to breeding in artificial nestboxes, a useful substitute for natural nest holes.

Identification Unmistakable, with blue cap, black and white face pattern, green back and yellow belly. Much smaller than Great Tit, which is black on the head.

Habits Cheeky and confident, often barging to the front of the queue of birds to take food, endearing it to many householders. In winter forms flocks with other tit species, which do a circuit of gardens to maximise their ability to find food.

Adult

Feeding During nesting time feeds mainly on insects, especially caterpillars. In autumn and winter will also take seeds and peanuts.

Juvenile

Breeding A hole nester, building a nest from grass lined with moss and feathers, and laying from 5–16 (usually 10–12) white eggs with a few spots, incubated for 13–16 days. Young fledge after 16–22 days. One brood.

Voice A variety of chattering calls and song, with trills and scolding sounds, often used as contact calls with other members of a flock.

When & where Resident. Found throughout Britain and Ireland apart from extreme north and west. Very common in gardens. Currently on the increase.

GREAT TIT

Parus major

The largest European tit is widespread and common in Britain, thanks partly to the efforts of householders providing extra supplies of food and nestboxes where this former woodland species can breed in safety. Like their smaller relatives, Great Tits have adapted well to living alongside humans, and are thriving as a result.

Identification Arguably the smartest and most brightly coloured of its family, with black head and throat, white cheeks, green back and bright lemon-yellow underparts bisected by a black bar (thicker in the male than the female).

Habits A noticeable, far from shy species, always amongst the first to feed if you provide a feeding station. In spring and early summer males sing their repetitive two-note song from prominent perches.

Feeding During the breeding season feeds mainly on insects, especially large caterpillars, but outside this time will take seeds and peanuts from artificial feeders.

Breeding Builds a nest in a hole in a tree or, more often in gardens, a nestbox. Lays 5–11 white eggs with reddish spots, incubated for 11–15 days. Young fledge after 3 weeks. One, sometimes two, broods.

Voice The repetitive and strident 'tea-cher, tea-cher' is its best known sound; along with a bewilderingly wide variety of other calls.

When & where Resident. Found throughout Britain and Ireland apart from extreme north and west. Very common in gardens. Currently increasing, thanks in part to mild winters.

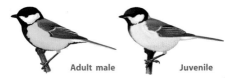

Adult male   Juvenile

NUTHATCH

Sitta europaea

This common but often overlooked woodland bird has a unique feature: it is the only British species able to climb down the trunks and branches of trees as well as up. In recent years it has adapted well to artificial feeders, and is now a regular visitor to many larger gardens, especially those near woods and forests.

Identification Seen well, the Nuthatch is unmistakable simply by its actions. Steel-blue upperparts, orange underparts and black 'bandit mask' also highly distinctive. Often resembles a small woodpecker.

Feeding Usually first seen clambering around the trunk or large branches of a tree. In spring, males sing from a prominent perch on the end of a branch. Look out for its acrobatic ability to climb vertically downwards.

Feeding Feeds mainly on insects in the breeding season, and seeds and nuts in autumn and winter. Will regularly visit bird tables and seed and nut feeders.

Breeding Nests in holes in trees, laying 6–8 white eggs spotted with red, incubated for 13–18 days. Young fledge after 23–24 days. One brood.

Male, N Europe

Male, Britain &
W Europe

Female

Juvenile

Voice Loud, echoing 'pee-uu' call, often the best way to detect the bird's presence, especially in spring.

When & where Resident, and fairly sedentary. Common in mixed and deciduous woodland throughout England and Wales apart from parts of eastern England. A few breed in southern Scotland. Absent from Ireland. Currently increasing and extending its range northwards, probably due to global warming.

TREECREEPER

Certhia familiaris

There can hardly be any British bird which has such an appropriate and descriptive name: this species is invariably glimpsed as it crawls, mouse like, around trunks and branches of trees, in search of its insect prey.

Identification With its unique tree climbing habits it cannot really be confused with any other bird. Much smaller and slimmer than Nuthatch or any woodpeckers, with brown upperparts, whitish underparts shading to brown on flanks, and long, decurved bill. Unlike Nuthatch, is not able to climb down tree trunks.

Habits As its name suggests, spends most of its life creeping up and along tree bark, probing for tiny morsels of food with its delicate, thin bill. Rarely flies anything but a very short distance from tree to tree.

Adult

Juvenile

Feeding Feeds entirely on small insects and grubs taken from the surface of or beneath the bark of trees.

Breeding Nests inside a crack or crevice in a tree, laying 5–6 white eggs with a few brownish spots, incubated for 13–15 days. Young fledge after 14–16 days. One, but also often two, broods. Will occasionally breed in special wedge shaped artificial nestbox if placed in suitable habitat.

Voice A thin, very high pitched trill, easily overlooked. Call a high pitched 'tsee'.

When & where Resident and highly sedentary. Found in most British and Irish woods, though absent from the extreme north and west of Britain. Currently increasing thanks to mild winters.

JAY

Garrulus glandarius

Perhaps because of its bright plumage and secretive behaviour, the Jay does not share the Magpie's status as public enemy number one – even though like its cousin it also takes the eggs and chicks of breeding songbirds to supplement its diet.

Identification Seen well, cannot be mistaken for any other species. A large pigeon-sized bird, with mainly pinkish brown plumage, which can appear different shades depending on the

prevailing light. Also has black and white speckled crest and distinctive blue patch on wing; in flight shows white rump.

Habits For its size, quite a shy and secretive bird, especially during the breeding season. Often seen in flight, when its shape and bounding flight action are distinctive even at some distance. Will sometimes visit bird tables in search of nuts.

Feeding Like other members of the crow family, Jays will eat a wide variety of food including acorns, insects and birds' eggs and chicks.

Breeding Builds a cup-shaped nest from twigs, often placed in a tree fork, laying 5–8 pale olive coloured eggs shaded with brown speckles, incubated for 16–17 days. Young fledge after 19–23 days. One brood.

Voice A harsh screech; also a mewing call rather like that of the Buzzard.

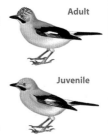

Adult

Juvenile

When & where Resident, with continental immigrants boosting numbers in autumn and winter. Found throughout England, Wales and southern Scotland; also thinly spread in Ireland. Currently increasing.

MAGPIE

Pica pica

The bird which people either love or hate, the Magpie has become something of a pantomime villain in the past few years, as it has been unfairly blamed on the decline of songbirds. Others regard it as a handsome and intelligent bird.

Identification An unmistakable bird, apparently black and white until a closer view reveals subtle shades of

blue and green on the wings and tail. Wings are rounded, enabling it to fly through dense foliage; tail long and graduated for the same reason.

Habits A noisy, sociable member of the crow family, easily seen and heard, making it appear that there are more Magpies than there actually are. Birds often squabble amongst themselves.

Juvenile

Adult

Feeding Despite its reputation, feeds mainly on insects, nuts and any other scraps it can find, often scavenging road kills. During the breeding season will also raid nests to take chicks and eggs.

Breeding Builds a large, untidy nest from loose twigs, often easily visible in a tree. Lays 5–8 pale bluish green eggs with reddish blotches, incubated for 17–18 days. Young (which often leave the nest before their tail has fully grown!) fledge after 22–28 days. One brood.

Voice A loud, harsh and familiar rattle, like a child imitating a machine gun!

When & where Resident. Found throughout England, Wales and Ireland, and in parts of eastern and southern Scotland. Currently increasing, probably because it is so well adapted to living alongside human beings.

JACKDAW

Corvus monedula

The smallest British crow, and a firm favourite for its cheeky appearance and sociable behaviour. Like the other members of its family, it is highly intelligent and adaptable, and has learned quickly to take advantage of human beings.

Identification Much smaller than Rook and Carrion Crow, with blackish upperparts, greyish underparts, and a distinctive pale grey patch around the back of the head and neck. Short bill and beady eye. In flight appears smaller and shorter winged than other crows, and is usually identified by its distinctive 'chacking' call.

Habits A sociable bird, it often gathers in flocks (sometimes alongside other crow species) to feed, especially in seed fields or open grassy areas. May also be seen in large, noisy flocks flying to roost just before dusk, especially in autumn and winter.

Feeding Feeds on a wide variety of plant and animal items, and will readily come to bird tables and feeding stations.

Breeding Normally nests in a hole in a tree or stone wall, building a loose nest from sticks, and laying 4–6 pale bluish green eggs, with dark blotches, incubated for 17–18 days. Young fledge after 4–5 weeks. One brood.

Voice A distinctive 'chak', often followed by a gentler second note, usually uttered in flight.

When & where Resident. Common throughout rural and suburban areas of England, Wales, and southern and eastern Scotland. Very common in Ireland. Currently increasing.

Adult

Juvenile

CARRION CROW

Corvus corone

The classic 'black' crow, often regarded as almost as much of a villain as its black and white cousin the Magpie. Lively, intelligent and adaptable, the Carrion Crow is destined to thrive in the 21st century.

Identification The only completely black bird commonly seen in Britain – the Raven is generally confined to upland areas. Distinguished from the Rook by its all black face and bill, and bulkier appearance. In flight the long, broad wings and thick set body give it a fearsome appearance.

Habits Noisy, sociable and liable to bully smaller birds out of the way, especially when food is at stake. Often visits gardens.

Feeding Feeds on almost anything! For example: seeds, insects, road kills, eggs, baby birds, bread, and unmentionable items scavenged from waste sites. Thrives on our wasteful society.

Breeding Builds a large, untidy nest from twigs, often high in the branches of a tree, and easily visible (crows have few enemies!) Lays 4–6 pale bluish green eggs, with reddish brown blotches, incubated for 17–21 days. Young fledge after 4–5 weeks. One brood.

Voice A harsh cawing sound, often uttered in flight.

When & where Resident. Widely distributed throughout urban and rural habitats in England, Wales and southern and eastern Scotland. In north and west Scotland and most of Ireland it is replaced by the Hooded Crow, now regarded as a full species. Currently increasing.

Adult hybrid

Adult Carrion

Adult Hooded

STARLING

Sturnus vulgaris

One of the most familiar yet often overlooked town and garden birds, the Starling is also one of the most attractive and fascinating, with complex social behaviour – and when seen in close up, a stunningly iridescent plumage.

Identification At first sight a dull brownish black bird; but take a closer look and you will see greenish sheen to the dark plumage, and in breeding season tiny pale spots and streaks. Juvenile Starlings often puzzle observers, as they are brown and nondescript; but have a similar shape and habits to the adults.

Habits Sociable, almost always seen in large, noisy flocks, squabbling amongst each other for food. Very familiar in gardens, adapting readily to obtaining food from all kinds of different sources.

Feeding Fairly catholic in taste, and able to feed on seeds and nuts provided by ourselves. Natural food includes invertebrates on lawns and grassy fields, obtained by probing with its sharp bill.

Breeding Usually nests in a hole in a tree, wall or building, laying 4–7 pale blue eggs, incubated for 12–15 days. Young fledge after 3 weeks. One or two broods.

Voice Starlings are great mimics, able to imitate many other birds as well as artificial sounds such as mobile phones and car alarms!

Adult Male

When & where Resident, with continental immigrants in autumn and winter. Common throughout Britain and Ireland apart from the extreme highlands. Currently decreasing for largely unknown reasons.

Juvenile

HOUSE SPARROW   *Passer domesticus*

Our most familiar bird is sadly nothing like as common as it once was, and has disappeared from some areas – notably from the centre of London. Nevertheless it is still a common enough sight in much of urban, suburban and rural Britain.

Identification With their neat black bib, grey and brown cap and cheeky demeanour, males are hard to mistake for anything else. Females and young birds more nondescript in appearance, with pale buff underparts, streaked brown upperparts and a clear pale stripe behind the eye.

Habits Usually seen around human habitation. Sociable and gregarious, often gathering in small

flocks to feed and socialise. Used to living alongside humans and a ready visitor to garden feeding stations.

Feeding Feeds on a variety of seeds and grains, and will also take nuts from feeders and other kitchen scraps. In breeding season feeds young on insects.

Breeding Builds its nest close to human dwellings or other buildings, often under the eaves. Lays 3–6 pale eggs with brown and grey speckles, incubated for 11–14 days. Young fledge after 14–19 days. May have three or even four broods in a single season. Often nests in small colonies of up to a dozen or more pairs.

Voice A characteristic chirping – a familiar sound of built-up areas.

When & where Resident. Still common throughout Britain and Ireland apart from the highlands and offshore islands. Currently undergoing unexplained decline.

Male   Female

CHAFFINCH

Fringilla coelebs

One of our commonest breeding birds, the Chaffinch is found throughout rural Britain, and in some parts of the countryside outnumbers all other species. In recent years has also adapted well to take advantage of food and nest sites provided by keen gardeners.

Identification With his bright orange-pink underparts, grey head and white wing bars, the male is unlikely to be confused with any other species (apart perhaps from the brighter pink Bullfinch, which has a black head). Females a dull version of the male, with buffish below.

Habits A sociable bird, though in the breeding season males defend their territory by singing their rather monotonous song throughout the day.

Juvenile

Frequent visitor to gardens, either feeding on the lawn or taking seed and nuts from feeders.

Feeding Feeds mainly on seeds, grains and in gardens on peanuts. During the breeding season prefers insect food.

Breeding Builds a neat nest in the fork of a tree, laying 3–5 pale blue eggs with darker spots, incubated for 11–13 days. Young fledge after 12–15 days. One or two broods.

Voice A distinctive song, described as sounding like a fast bowler running up to make a delivery! Variety of calls including 'pink'.

When & where Resident, though in autumn and winter visitors from continental Europe add to the resident population. Common and widespread in almost all parts of Britain and Ireland, apart from the extremes of the highlands and islands. Currently increasing.

Adult

BRAMBLING

Fringilla montifringilla

The northern European equivalent of the more familiar Chaffinch, the Brambling mainly visits this country in autumn and winter, and is best looked for in beech woods, where they search for their favourite food of beech mast.

Summer female

Identification Males look like even brighter version of the Chaffinch: but black head, orange underparts and in flight the white rump are distinctive. Females also brightly coloured, but streakier and with less black on head than male. Juvenile birds are paler and greyer on head and less bright below.

Habits A sociable bird, usually seen in flocks during the winter. Often associates with other seed eaters such as finches and buntings. Will sometimes visit gardens, especially in rural areas near large areas of broadleaved or mixed woodland.

Feeding Feeds almost exclusively on seeds during the autumn and winter months, and will take advantage of feeding stations in gardens, often hopping about beneath the feeder to pick up spilt seed.

Breeding Only a few pairs nest in Britain each year. The rest head north and east to Scandinavia.

Summer Male   **Winter Male**   **Summer female**   **Juvenile**

Voice Two calls: a gentle 'chuck-chuck', and a harsher, squeaky 'wee-eek'.

When & where Autumn and winter visitor, arriving in September and October and departing in March and April. Found in many parts of Britain, though thinly distributed so may be hard to find. Scarce in Ireland. More likely to visit gardens during harsh winter weather.

GREENFINCH

Carduelis chloris

One of the commonest and most widespread members of the finch family, the Greenfinch is also a very common visitor to gardens, often staying on to breed there.

Identification Adult male bright yellow-green, with a pale grey tinge on the wings and darker grey on the wingtips and tail. Female slightly less bright. Both have pale ivory coloured bill. In flight yellow on wings becomes obvious. Juveniles can look almost sparrow-like, as they lack most of the green and yellow pigments in their plumage.

Habits In breeding season males often seen singing in a display flight, or from a high perch in a tree. In late

Male   **Female**   **Juvenile**

summer, autumn and winter form
flocks, often visiting bird feeding
stations, where they have a particular
preference for sunflower seeds.

Feeding During the breeding season
Greenfinches mainly feed on seeds and
insects, while in winter they also take peanuts.

Breeding Often nests in colonies of several pairs,
building a cup-shaped nest deep in the foliage of a
tree or dense bush, such as a cypress. Lays 3–6 pale
eggs with darker spots, incubated for 12–14 days.
Young fledge after 13–17 days. Two broods.

Voice A variety of wheezing and twittering calls. Song
a combination of trills, whistles and twitters rather like
that of a Canary.

When & where Resident. Common and widespread
throughout Britain apart from northern and western
Scotland; less widespread in Ireland. Currently on the
increase.

GOLDFINCH

Carduelis carduelis

One of our most attractive and charming finches – an appropriate adjective since a flock of Goldfinches was once known as a 'charm'! Once popular with the cagebird trade, Goldfinches are holding their own in the modern world.

Identification Adults unmistakable, with buffish, black and white plumage, a bright crimson face patch, and golden yellow stripes on the wings which flash brightly when the birds take to the air. Juveniles appear mainly brownish buff until they fly, when they also reveal the bright yellow stripes across the wing.

Habits A sociable little bird which is usually seen in pairs or small flocks. To feed, Goldfinches perch on the tops of thistles, teasels and other spiky plants to remove the seeds.

Adult

Juvenile

Feeding Feeds mainly on tiny seeds, removed from plants using its specially pointed and conical bill. In recent years has taken to feeding on sunflower seeds from artificial feeders, so look out for them in your garden!

Breeding Builds a small, cup-shaped nest in the outer branches or twigs of a tree or bush. Lays 4–6 pale eggs with dark spots and streaks, incubated for 12–14 days. Young fledge after 12–15 days. Two or three broods.

Voice Musical twittering songs and calls, with trills, creating a delightful sound.

When & where Resident. Common and fairly widespread throughout England, Wales and parts of southern and eastern Scotland, and also found in parts of Ireland. Currently increasing.

SISKIN

Carduelis spinus

This tiny little finch was once a specialist of coniferous woodlands, but during the late 20th century it adapted to life in our gardens, where today it is a common and frequent visitor. Often appears in the company of its cousin the Redpoll, in mixed flocks.

Identification Like a smaller, streakier and darker version of the Greenfinch. Males have a black cap and bib, yellowish green breast and streaky black and green upperparts. Females more subdued, with less black on head. Juveniles brown and streaky.

Habits Often seen in flocks, and especially keen on seed and nut feeders in gardens. Conifers also help attract this species, and may even persuade them to nest.

Feeding Mainly feeds on seeds and insects, but also takes peanuts and sunflower seeds.

Breeding Breeds mainly away from gardens in conifer plantations and mixed woodlands. Lays 3–6 pale bluish white eggs, incubated for 11–14 days. Young fledge after 13–15 days. Two broods.

Voice Song a rapid series of twitters, trills and wheezy notes, rather like that of Greenfinch. Also a number of wheezy calls.

When & where Resident, though often commoner in gardens in late autumn, winter and especially early spring, when males may even begin to sing during sunny weather. Fairly widespread throughout Britain and Ireland in autumn and winter, though during the breeding season more common in the west and north. Currently doing very well.

Male

Female

Juvenile

LINNET

Carduelis cannabina

Once a common bird of farmland and heathland areas, the Linnet has undergone a major decline in the past few decades, probably due to the lack of seeds available on farmland in winter. May still be seen in gardens, however, especially those near weedy fields.

Identification A small, neat finch, which in autumn and winter appears mainly buffish brown with paler flashes on the wings in flight. During the breeding season, however, the male adopts a stunning rose pink hue to his forehead and breast.

Female

Habits Outside the breeding season Linnets travel in pairs, family parties or small flocks in search of food, and may cover a wide area.

Feeding Feeds mainly on insects during the spring and summer, while outside these seasons changes to a diet of seeds.

Breeding Builds a cup-shaped nest from grass, usually lined with hair and feathers, in dense foliage in a bush or shrub. Lays 4–6 pale eggs, overlaid with faint marks which look like pencil scribbles! Incubates

for 10–14 days. Young fledge after 11–13 days. Two, sometimes three, broods.

Adult male

Juvenile

Voice The Linnet's song is a delightful, melodious series of twitters and whistles, which made it deservedly popular as a Victorian cagebird. Call a soft twitter, often uttered in flight as it passes overhead.

When & where Resident. Still fairly widespread in England and Wales, and also found in parts of lowland Scotland and Ireland. Currently decreasing.

LESSER REDPOLL

Carduelis cabaret

Recently 'split' from several species of redpoll found in northern and western Europe, the Lesser Redpoll has undergone a rapid decline recently, again mainly due to lack of seeds on farmland.

Identification A small, streaky finch: appears mainly buffish brown, with darker back and wings. Adults always show the crimson patch on the forehead that gives the species its name. During the breeding season males also have a pink breast, and this may still show, though less brightly, in autumn and winter. Juveniles brown and streaky.

Habits A sociable bird, almost always seen in flocks, often in the company of Siskins. In winter prefers wooded areas near running water where insects are likely to be more numerous. An occasional visitor to gardens.

Feeding Feeds mainly on seeds and insects, and will occasionally come to seed feeders in gardens.

Breeding Breeds mainly in birch and alder woodlands and on heathland, away from gardens. Lays 4–5 pale blue eggs with darker markings, incubated for 10–14 days. Young fledge after 11–14 days. One or two broods.

Male

Voice Song a selection of rapid, staccato notes like typewriter keys; also gives a range of trills and whistling calls, often in flight.

Juvenile

When & where Resident. Breeding strongholds are mainly in northern and western Britain; also found in parts of Ireland. In autumn and winter more widely scattered, though thinly so. Currently decreasing rapidly.

BULLFINCH

Pyrrhula pyrrhula

Once a common sight along our country hedgerows, this stunning finch has, along with other seed-eating birds, suffered a rapid and severe decline in numbers. This is almost certainly caused by a lack of food in autumn and winter, due to modern farming methods.

Identification Seen well, male unmistakable, with his black cap, grey back and bright cherry pink underparts. Female a monochrome version of male, being brownish below. In flight both sexes show a distinctive white rump, especially obvious as they fly away!

Habits A shy species, easily flushed when alarmed. Tends to feed quietly in a bush, and often best located by its call: a soft 'piu'.

Feeding Feeds mainly on seeds, crushed in its large bill. Also enjoys buds of fruit trees, making it an agricultural pest in some areas.

Adult male   **Adult female**   **Juvenile**

Breeding Builds its nest deep inside a bush or foliage of a tree, making a loose nest from small twigs lined with hair and grass. Lays 3–6 pale blue eggs with fine black spots, incubated for 12–14 days. Young fledge after 15–17 days. Two, sometimes three, broods.

Voice A gentle, piping 'piu'. Song an extended version of this, with additional wheezing and piping notes.

When & where Resident. Now scarce across much of its former range, though still found throughout most of Britain and Ireland apart from the extreme north and west. Currently undergoing major decline.

HAWFINCH *Coccothraustes coccothraustes*

Britain's largest species of finch is a magnificent bird, with a thick, heavy bill capable of exerting enormous pressure to crush its favourite food of cherry stones!

Identification Rarely seen well, but when good views are obtained hard to confuse with any other species. Larger and even more thick-set than Bullfinch, and much larger and more rust coloured than Chaffinch. Adult male has rusty orange head and underparts, a grey patch around the neck, and dark

back. Female duller. In flight shows prominent black and white wing pattern.

Habits Very shy and unobtrusive, often hiding deep within the foliage of mature trees. Will occasionally visit gardens, especially in rural areas near mature broad-leaved woodland.

Feeding Feeds mainly on seeds and berries, such as cherries and beech nuts, which it crushes using its enormous and powerful bill.

Adult female

Breeding Builds a cup-shaped nest from small twigs lined with hair or grass, usually in dense foliage in woodland. Lays 4–5 pale bluish white eggs with dark spots, incubated for 11–13 days. Young fledge after 10–14 days. One brood.

Voice Best located by its very loud flight call: an explosive 'zik'.

When & where Resident. Found in suitable habitat (i.e. mature woodlands with beech or hornbeam) in southern England and parts of East Anglia; also a few north to the Scottish borders. Rare in Wales and absent from Ireland. Currently in decline.

Juvenile

YELLOWHAMMER   *Emberiza citrinella*

This stunning member of the bunting family has, along with so many other seed-eating species dependent on farmland, suffered extreme declines in the past 50 years or so. Nevertheless it can still be encountered in many rural areas, as it sings its well known song.

Female

Identification Breeding males unmistakable: our only bright yellow bird apart from the two species of wagtail. Yellow head, face and underparts contrast with streaked brownish upperparts. Winter males and females duller brown with yellowish streaks. In flight reveals a plain, unstreaked chestnut rump.

Habits A familiar bird of farmland fields and hedgerows, especially where there are plenty of weed seeds to feed on in autumn and winter. Often seen perched on the top twig of a hedgerow. Breeds quite late so males often sing well into late summer.

Male

Juvenile

Feeding Feeds mainly on seeds and berries in winter, though switches to insects in spring and summer. Will occasionally visit artificial seed feeders in gardens.

Breeding Builds a substantial nest in a hedge or bank. Lays 3–5 pale eggs with darker spots, incubated for 11–14 days. Young fledge after 12–13 days. Two or three broods.

Voice Song unmistakable: the famous 'a little bit of bread and no cheeeese'!

When & where Resident. Following population crash, now widely but thinly distributed across England, Wales and lowland Scotland. Scarce but widely found in Ireland. Currently in rapid decline.

REED BUNTING   *Emberiza schoeniclus*

Superficially resembling a House Sparrow, this attractive little bunting has also declined in recent years, due to food shortages on farmland. However, at the same time it has taken to visiting gardens on a more regular basis than before, so may paradoxically be easier to see.

Juvenile

Identification Male has smart black head, face and bib, with thin grey line dividing bib from rest of face. Brown, streaky upperparts and pale greyish white underparts. Females and winter males less obvious, with subtle but distinctive face pattern.

Habits Like most finches and buntings prefers to feed in flocks in autumn and winter, often in the company of other species. In breeding season usually found near water, with males perched on crops or reeds to deliver their song.

Feeding Feeds mainly on seeds, though will also take insects in breeding season. In recent years this species has learned to come to bird tables and seed feeders in gardens.

Breeding Breeds mainly in farm crops or reed beds, laying 4–5 olive coloured eggs with darker spots and blotches, incubated for 12–14 days. Young fledge after 10–13 days. Two, occasionally three, broods.

Voice A monotonous, flatly toned call and song, consisting of the same note repeated at brief intervals, in a hesitant and rather bored manner!

When & where Resident. Widely if sometimes thinly distributed across England, Wales, lowland Scotland and Ireland. Currently decreasing.

Adult female

GREAT CRESTED GREBE

Podiceps cristatus

Our largest grebe, once persecuted for its plumes and feathers, but now safe to live in peace. A frequent sight on ponds, rivers and lakes.

Identification A slender, elegant waterbird with brown upperparts, pale underparts and during the breeding season a prominent crest. In winter appears paler.

Habits Usually seen swimming on surface; or diving for food. Breeding display complex and spectacular.

Feeding & breeding Feeds mainly on fish obtained by diving. Makes floating nest, and often covers eggs with water weed to hide them from predators. Chicks ride on parents' back during early life.

Voice Variety of loud, nasal calls, often given in display.

When & where Common on suitable waterways in most of England apart from south west; also parts of Wales, southern Scotland and Ireland. Resident.

LITTLE GREBE

Tachybaptus ruficollis

Our smallest grebe, which although fairly common, often skulks on the edge of ponds making it harder to see. Also known as the Dabchick.

Identification Tiny – at first sight can be mistaken for a young waterbird. Short bill, fluffy back end and dark brown plumage.

Habits Usually seen swimming near edge of water, near the safety of reeds or other vegetation. Dives beneath surface for food.

Feeding & breeding Feeds on invertebrates such as molluscs and small fish, obtained by diving. Builds floating nest near edge of water, usually by vegetation.

Voice Rapid, staccato call – sounds like high pitched laughing.

When & where On ponds and lakes throughout lowland Britain. Resident.

CORMORANT

Phalacrocorax carbo

Once mainly a coastal species, the Cormorant has spread inland – especially outside the breeding season when it may be seen on rivers and lakes.

Identification A large, black bird with broad wings and a long neck. Seen closely, yellowish face patch and variable white on belly are obvious.

Habits Often sits in a small group, drying its wings. Also seen in flight overhead, or diving for food.

Feeding & breeding Feeds mainly on fish, obtained by deep diving. Builds large, untidy nest from twigs, usually in colonies.

Voice Throaty calls uttered at nest site; otherwise mainly silent.

When & where On rivers, lakes and large ponds and in areas near the coast throughout Britain and Ireland. Resident.

MUTE SWAN

Cygnus olor

Europe's largest flying bird, and celebrated for its royal connections, Mute Swans are haughty, sometimes aggressive creatures, with little fear of humans.

Identification Unmistakable! Huge white bird with orange bill. Males have larger black 'knob' above bill. Cygnets grey, moulting to variable amounts of white.

Habits Generally seen floating serenely along a river or surface of a lake. In flight makes a whirring noise with its wings.

Feeding & breeding Feeds on small aquatic vegetation obtained by dipping neck beneath water. Also grazes in wet fields. Also takes bread – but don't get too close to that snapping bill!

Voice Generally silent – apart from hissing if approached!

When & where Common throughout lowland Britain and Ireland, generally on open water, especially park lakes and rivers. Resident.

CANADA GOOSE   *Branta canadensis*

Originally introduced from North America as ornamental waterfowl, the Canada Goose has adapted well to modern life, and is a familiar sight in many towns and cities.

Identification Large goose with mainly brown plumage (paler beneath), and distinctive black neck and head with white face patch.

Habits Sociable and noisy; often gathering in flocks to feed. Can be aggressive towards other waterfowl.

Feeding & breeding Feeds mainly by grazing on grass and other vegetation, often in parks. Builds large nest by side of water or nearby.

Voice Loud, deep honking call, often uttered in flight.

When & where Common and widespread in any suitable habitat throughout England and Wales; scarce in Scotland, and in one or two places in Ireland. Resident.

GREYLAG GOOSE

Anser anser

Originally confined to north-west Scotland, the Greylag Goose has recently spread throughout Britain via feral birds, and in some parts is as common as its cousin the Canada Goose.

Identification The classic large 'grey' goose: in fact mainly brown, with orange bill and pale under tail. In flight looks thick necked and bulky.

Habits Gathers in large, noisy flocks, grazing and loafing about on or near the water.

Feeding & breeding
Feeds mainly on plant material, either obtained from beneath the water or by grazing.

Voice A loud, raucous honking – the classic goose sound!

When & where
Nowadays found in suitable habitat throughout eastern Britain, and in other parts of the country where feral birds have managed to spread. Resident.

EGYPTIAN GOOSE *Alopochen aegyptiacus*

This peculiar looking bird is related to the Shelducks rather than the true geese. It is another ornamental species of waterfowl which has 'gone native'.

Identification Strange combination of brownish plumage, white grey and chestnut on wing, and peculiar mask-like face pattern. In flight reveals white wing patches.

Habits Tends to spend a lot of time doing little apart from feeding or sleeping!

Feeding & breeding Feeds mainly on vegetation. Breeds earlier than many geese.

Voice Weird range of quacks, hisses and trumpeting calls. Generally silent while feeding.

When & where Originally released into the wild in Norfolk, has now spread throughout East Anglia and into surrounding counties, including parts of south-east England and the Midlands. A few may be seen elsewhere. Resident.

MALLARD

Anas platyrhynchos

The classic 'duck' which every child is taken to feed, the Mallard is a handsome bird – especially the male.

Identification Male has bottle green head, white collar magenta and grey plumage with blue 'speculum' on folded wing. Female various shades of subtle brown and black markings.

Habits Usually seen in pairs or flocks. In breeding season several males can attack a female – a violent and unpleasant sight. In summer sit around and moult.

Feeding & breeding
Omnivorous, taking plant and animal food – and of course 'bread for the ducks'!

Voice Female has familiar quack. Male's call a quieter grunt or wheeze.

When & where Common and widespread throughout Britain and Ireland – even on offshore islands and at the coast. Resident.

SHOVELER

Anas clypeata

Named for its extraordinary spatulate bill, which it uses to sieve tiny morsels of food from just beneath the water surface.

Identification Superficially like a Mallard: but bill always distinctive. Male has green head, white belly and rusty flanks; female brown with darker wingtips.

Habits Sociable and gregarious. Generally feeds by swimming rather than grazing on land.

Feeding & breeding Feeds on wide range of plant and animal food, obtained by specialised sieving technique while swimming. Scarce breeder in Britain.

Voice Fairly quiet – occasional soft quacks.

When & where Small British breeding population augmented by immigrant birds in autumn and winter, when most likely to be seen on lakes and other water bodies. Mainly found in southern and eastern Britain.

WIGEON

Anas penelope

This delightful duck is a common autumn and winter visitor to Britain, where it can easily find food by grazing.

Identification Male distinctive: with orange brown head and yellowish forehead, pinkish breast, grey body and black under tail. Female various shades of chestnut and brown – best identified by bill shape.

Habits Unlike many ducks, often grazes in grassy fields. Very sociable, often calling to each other even while feeding.

Feeding & breeding Feeds almost entirely on plant material, obtained by ducking its head below water or grazing. Scarce breeder in Britain.

Voice Male gives distinctive and evocative whistling call, often in flight.

When & where In autumn and winter found on suitable large areas of water and grazing marsh throughout lowland Britain and Ireland – often near the coasts.

GADWALL

Anas strepera

This superficially grey looking duck in fact has a beautifully marked plumage, with subtle markings of black and brown. Often overlooked.

Identification Male has subtle markings known as vermiculations revealed on a close view, black under tail and smaller bill than Mallard. Female smaller and more delicate than Mallard.

Habits Usually 'dabbles' for food just beneath the water surface. Sometimes hangs around with Coots and diving ducks and picks disturbed morsels of food off the surface as they dive.

Feeding & breeding Feeds mainly on tiny morsels of plant matter. Scarce breeder in Britain.

Voice Male has deep croak; female a more chattering quack.

When & where In autumn and winter found on shallow, open water throughout south-east England, East Anglia and the Midlands; occasional though scarce elsewhere.

TEAL

Anas crecca

Our smallest duck, often flushed from its hiding place in a small patch of water, marsh or flooded field.

Identification Male stunning: with chestnut head, green eye-patch, grey body and yellow patch under tail. Female basically brown with darker markings. Both have green speculum on edge of wing.

Habits Often skulks out of sight, hiding in dense vegetation on the edge of water before flying away on fast beating wings.

Feeding & breeding Feeds on wide range of animal and plant items, by grazing or dabbling. Nests on ground in thick vegetation, always near water.

Voice Male gives high-pitched whistle.

When & where Breeds mainly in northern Britain, though also a few in the south. Much more widespread outside the breeding season.

TUFTED DUCK

Aythya fuligula

The commonest and best known diving duck in Britain, numbers of breeding birds are swamped by immigrants from northern Europe and Siberia in autumn and winter.

Identification Male very distinctive: the only common black duck with white patches on its sides. Female brown, with paler patches. Both have tuft on back of head.

Habits Usually found on open, deeper water where it can dive for food.

Feeding & breeding Feeds on a wide variety of animal and plant items obtained by diving, and also by grazing ashore. Nests on ground or in water.

Voice Fairly quiet – various calls when breeding.

When & where In autumn and winter found commonly on waterways throughout lowland Britain and some parts of Ireland. In breeding season far less numerous but still widespread.

POCHARD

Aythya ferina

Our other common diving duck is another primarily autumn and winter visitor to Britain, though a few stay to breed.

Identification Male a large, bulky and handsome duck, with a deep chestnut head, black belly and grey body. Female a dull greyish brown. Both have a large bill and sloping forehead.

Habits Usually found in large flocks on areas of deep, open water, where they can dive for food. Rarely seen elsewhere.

Feeding & breeding Feeds on wide range of plant and animal food. Scarce breeder in Britain.

Voice Calls mostly weak and hard to hear at any distance.

When & where In autumn and winter, common and widespread in eastern, southern and central Britain; scarcer or absent elsewhere.

MANDARIN DUCK _Aix galericulata_

This magnificent looking duck is another non-native, ornamental species, introduced into Britain in the 19th century to add a splash of colour to parks and gardens.

Identification Male a wonderful combination of shape and bright colours including green, orange and white, with 'sails' on back; female grey with paler markings.

Habits A fairly shy bird, though when used to humans will venture close for food.

Feeding & breeding Feeds on wide range of plant and animal food obtained in various ways. Nests in holes in trees, from which young must leap to the ground!

Voice Various whistling calls, generally used in courtship.

When & where Mainly confined to south-east England, near where the original feral population was first released. Resident.

RUDDY DUCK

Oxyura jamaicensis

Yet another non-native species of duck – this time accidentally introduced in the mid 20th century when a few of this North American species escaped from captivity.

Identification Males unmistakable, with bright rufous plumage, white cheeks, black cap and blue bill! Females browner, with dark cap. Both have 'stiff' tail sticking up at angle.

Habits A diving duck, found in pairs or small flocks. Prefers large areas of water in winter; smaller lakes in summer.

Feeding & breeding Feeds on insect larvae and aquatic plants found by diving. Nests in dense vegetation.

Voice Mainly silent, but during display male utters rattling sounds.

When & where Main stronghold the English Midlands, but also found in south-east England, the north-east, and a few places in Wales and Ireland. Resident.

COMMON BUZZARD

Buteo buteo

Our commonest large bird of prey has made something of a comeback in recent years, after decades of persecution and poisoning.

Identification Large, bulky raptor, brownish overall though very variable in shade. Broad, rounded wings with long 'fingers'.

Habits Usually seen in soaring flight, or flapping lazily across the sky. Also perches on posts.

Feeding & breeding Feeds on a range of carrion and freshly killed animals such as rabbits. Nests in large, mature trees.

Voice A plaintive, far carrying mewing call, usually given in flight.

When & where Best looked for on warm, sunny days when flight is easier. Stronghold is the west country and Wales, but now spreading eastwards and can be seen almost anywhere in suitable habitat.

PEREGRINE

Falco peregrinus

Our largest and most powerful falcon is built for speed, enabling it to hunt its prey by stooping down onto it from a great height.

Identification Large and thick-set, with broadly based pointed wings and a deep chest. Gives impression of sheer power. Mainly dark upperparts and streaked underparts; dark face mask.

Habits Usually seen in hunting flight, chasing fast in pursuit of its prey.

Feeding & breeding Feeds mainly on birds caught in flight.

Voice Rarely calls apart from near nest.

When & where In breeding season mainly in upland areas; in autumn and winter heads down to lowland areas such as coastal marshes; also sometimes spends the winter in big cities, using buildings as a lookout post. Resident.

HOBBY

Falco subbuteo

A summer visitor from Africa, this slim, delicate falcon resembles the Swifts and Martins which it often hunts.

Identification Slimmer and much darker than Kestrel, with narrower, pointed wings and a very different flight action. Dark bluish upperparts and pale underparts streaked dark; rusty under tail.

Habits Often hunts in small groups, chasing and catching dragonflies or Martins in mid-air. Best looked for in evenings when insects and birds gather; often near water.

Feeding & breeding Feeds on a variety of bird and insects food, caught in flight. Breeds in tall trees.

Voice Rapid, repeated 'kew kew kew' call.

When & where Summer visitor, arriving April and leaving August-September. Found in suitable heathland o wetland habitat across most of southern England, especially the far south and east.

PHEASANT

Phasianus colchicus

Originally introduced from Asia to Britain by the Romans, the Pheasant has the dubious honour of being our most hunted gamebird, with millions being shot each year.

Identification Male unmistakable, with green head, rich rufous brown plumage, and very long tail. Female plumper, shorter tailed and less colourful, to aid camouflage.

Habits Often skulks around the edge of a field, or outside the shooting season ventures into the open.

Feeding & breeding
Feeds on wide variety of grains, seeds and various items picked up from the ground. Breeds in dense cover on the edge of a field or in a wood.

Voice Loud, car-carrying croaking call.

When & where Common and widespread throughout lowland Britain and Ireland apart from extreme north and west. Resident.

COOT
Fulica atra

Though superficially resembling a duck, a Coot is in fact a member of the rail family, which has adapted to swimming rather than walking. Has semi-webbed feet.

Identification The only all black waterbird, with a distinctive white bill and facial patch. Told from Moorhen by larger size and lack of red or yellow on bill.

Chicks have red on head which can be confusing.

Habits Mainly swims around shallow wetlands, dabbling or diving in search of food.

Feeding & breeding Feeds on all kinds of aquatic material, mainly plants. Builds floating nest of vegetation, often in full view.

Voice A series of odd but distinctive single note calls.

When & where Common throughout lowland Britain apart from extreme south-west and north and west Scotland. Resident.

COMMON GULL

Larus canus

Despite its name, not our most common gull either on the coasts or inland, though in autumn and winter is fairly widespread.

Identification A handsome, medium-sized gull with an all-white head and underparts and mid-grey back and wings with black wing tips. Greenish bill and legs.

Habits Often joins flocks of Black-headed Gulls to forage on playing fields or in gardens.

Feeding & breeding Feeds mainly on invertebrates and small fish, obtained from the land or water. Breeds in colonies in remote parts of northern Britain.

Voice A mewing call that gives it the alternative name 'Mew Gull'.

When & where In autumn and winter can be found throughout Britain, though commoner near coasts. Usually with other gull species.

HERRING GULL

Larus argentatus

The classic 'seagull': large, noisy and always looking for trouble! In recent years has moved into city centres to breed.

Identification A large gull, with a white head and underparts, pale grey back and pink legs – a useful identification feature. Bill yellow with red spot. Young appear various shades of brown.

Habits Gregarious and opportunistic, always on the lookout for an easy meal.

Feeding & breeding Feeds on almost anything – fish, roadkill, unmentionable stuff scavenged from rubbish dumps – a true 21st-century bird.

Voice The classic honking 'seagull' call.

When & where Breeds mainly on coasts, but a few now do so on city roofs, well inland. Commoner in winter when it joins other gulls in flocks. Resident.

LESSER BLACK-BACKED GULL

Larus fuscus

The Herring Gull's smaller, neater relative has also adapted well to living alongside human beings, and also nests on city centre roofs.

Identification A medium to large gull, with white head and underparts contrasting with dark back – sometimes almost black, otherwise dark grey. Yellow legs a good identification feature.

Habits A bit more fastidious than the Herring Gull, though still highly adaptable to living alongside humans.

Feeding & breeding Feeds on most things, including fish and scraps. Breeds mainly in colonies on coasts, but has recently colonised roofs in city centres.

Voice Similar to Herring Gull, but slightly deeper in tone.

When & where In winter found over much of southern Britain, especially near cities. Less marine than Herring Gull.

COMMON TERN   *Sterna hirundo*

Once a bird of the coasts this elegant summer visitor has adapted to nesting inland, using specially built rafts on reservoirs and gravel pits.

Identification A slim, elegant bird, superficially gull like but much more graceful. Black cap, pale grey wings and black and white underparts; long tail streamers.

Habits Hunts by flying in buoyant manner over water in search of food, then plunging down to pick off the water surface.

Feeding & breeding Feeds mainly on small fish. Breeds in colonies on coast, and also on inland wetlands.

Voice Loud, high-pitched screech.

When & where Summer visitor, arriving in April and departing in September. Found mainly around our northern and eastern coasts, but also breeds inland in eastern and southern England.

SKYLARK

Alauda arvensis

The favourite bird of the poets is justly celebrated for its extraordinary song, delivered high in the sky during a prolonged song flight.

Identification Large, mainly brown songbird, with paler underparts and a raised crest. Usually seen in flight, and identified by its distinctive song.

Habits On the ground can be secretive and hard to see. Look for it in song-flight, where it may appear as a tiny speck high in the sky.

Feeding & breeding Feeds mainly on seeds, grain and insects. Breeds on the ground in arable farmland.

Voice Unmistakable outpouring of rich, powerful song, which seems to go on forever.

When & where A farmland species, formerly found throughout rural Britain, but has suffered heavy declines in recent years. Resident.

SAND MARTIN

Riparia riparia

One of the earliest spring migrants to arrive, coming in March and departing south to Africa in September. Usually seen over water.

Identification A small hirundine, told apart from House Martin by smaller size, all brown upperparts (no white rump) and white underparts with narrow brown band across chest.

Habits Flies low over water in search of insects. Nests in large, noisy colonies in sandbanks.

Feeding & breeding Feeds on small flying insects caught on the wing. Breeds in the banks of rivers or gravel pits, in burrow.

Voice A harsh twittering series of notes, delivered in flight.

When & where From early spring to autumn, anywhere near water where there is a suitable place to nest.

YELLOW WAGTAIL

Motacilla flava

An attractive and delicate summer visitor, which has declined in recent years due to the draining of marshy areas in the countryside.

Identification Bright yellow below, olive green above, with the characteristic long tail of its family. Told from Grey Wagtail by smaller size and lack of grey or black in plumage.

Habits Prefers damp areas such as wet meadows and marshes, especially around livestock where insects are common.

Feeding & breeding Feeds on small insects picked up from ground or by flycatching. Nests in shallow scrape on the ground.

Voice Call a long, drawn out 'tsweep'.

When & where Summer visitor, arriving April and departing August or September. Mainly found in eastern, central and southern England; a few in Wales.

MEADOW PIPIT

Anthus pratensis

The classic lbj – 'little brown job' – often overlooked, yet common and widespread throughout upland and lowland habitats across most of Britain.

Identification A small, slim songbird with a streaked brown plumage and thin bill. Best identified when flushed by thin, single note call.

Habits Unobtrusive except when males perform their song flight in the breeding season. In autumn and winter gathers in small flocks on open ground.

Feeding & breeding Feeds mainly on insects, and also takes seeds in autumn and winter. Builds cup-shaped nest from grasses, on ground.

Voice Call a thin 'seep', often given in flight; song a jumbled series of notes often delivered in parachuting song flight.

When & where Resident, found throughout Britain and Ireland in most habitats.

WILLOW WARBLER

Phylloscopus trochilus

Surprisingly perhaps, the Willow Warbler is our commonest summer visitor, with several million pairs making the long and arduous journey from southern Africa to breed each year.

Identification A small, delicate green and yellowish 'leaf warbler', with paler underparts, pale legs and a distinctive eye stripe. Best told apart from very similar Chiffchaff by distinctive song which descends down the scale.

Habits Lives in mixed or deciduous woodland or heathland, and often sings from a prominent perch in spring.

Feeding & breeding Feeds on small insects. Nests on ground, concealed in low vegetation.

Voice A beautiful, rather plaintive song, with a series of notes descending the scale.

When & where Summer visitor, April to September. Found throughout Britain and Ireland.

WHITE STORK *Ciconia ciconia*

A huge, stately bird, known to generations as the bringer of good luck – and babies! Following a decline across Europe is now making a comeback.

Identification Tall, statuesque and mainly white bird, with black wings and a large red bill.

Habits Often seen feeding in fields, alone or in small groups.

Feeding & breeding Feeds on wide variety of amphibians, beetles etc; builds huge nest of sticks on roofs, often using artificial platforms installed by the householder.

Voice Usually silent, apart from loud bill clattering when pair meets at nest.

When & where Summer visitor to much of southern and eastern Europe: commonest in Spain, Germany and eastern European countries where traditional farming still practised. Rare visitor to Britain.

HOOPOE

Upupa epops

This gaudy and unmistakable bird is a common summer visitor throughout continental Europe, which crosses the Channel annually to Britain, and occasionally stays to breed.

Identification Bright orange pink plumage, raised crest and black-and-white wings make this species unmistakable.

Habits A shy bird, often not seen until flushed as it feeds unobtrusively on the ground.

Feeding & breeding Feeds on wide range of items including large insects and lizards. Nests in hole in tree, and often discovered by the smell produced by its unhygienic habits.

Voice A distinctive, far-carrying and repetitive 'poo, poo, poo' which gives the species its name.

When & where Summer visitor to much of continental Europe, especially common in Spain and southern France. Annual visitor to southern Britain, usually in spring.

WRYNECK

Jynx torquilla

Once a common British breeding bird, this species has sadly declined to the point of extinction here, though it is still found commonly on the continent.

Identification A bizarre looking bird, related to the woodpeckers. Brown in appearance, though closer view reveals mottling and streaking with black and grey to resemble the bark of a tree.

Habits Seen mainly on ground, and if surprised will twist its neck and hiss like a snake!

Feeding & breeding Feeds mainly on ants taken directly from their nest. Breeds in hole in tree.

Voice Repeated 'kee-kee-kee', rather like a Kestrel.

When & where Summer visitor, found throughout continental Europe, but commonest in the east and Scandinavia. Scarce spring and autumn migrant to Britain, mainly on east coast.

CRESTED LARK

Galerida cristata

Despite breeding commonly just across the Channel in Calais, this species has hardly ever been recorded in Britain, due to its sedentary habits.

Identification Superficially similar to a Skylark, but with much longer, narrower crest.

Habits Like most larks seen mainly on the ground or in flight. Can allow quite close approach.

Feeding & breeding Feeds mostly on plant material including seeds, and a few invertebrates. Breeds on ground.

Voice Varied song full of long, fluty notes, and including mimicry of many other species.

When & where Sedentary and resident throughout much of continental Europe including Spain and northern France. Often seen on 'waste ground' by sides of road, where few other species choose to live. Very rare vagrant to Britain.

NIGHTINGALE   *Luscinia megarhynchos*

The legendary songster really does live up to its billing: delivering an extraordinary sound by day as well as by night.

Identification Hardly ever seen, so usually identified by song. An anonymous brown bird with few markings, and a distinctive rufous tail.

Habits Skulks deep inside dense bushes to deliver its song. Often sings through the night, but early in the season will also sing by day.

Feeding & breeding Feeds on invertebrates caught by foraging through leaf litter on ground. Breeds in dense foliage in scrub or woodland.

Voice A stunning and varied collection of remarkable sounds – must be heard to be appreciated!

When & where Summer visitor, widespread in southern and western Europe. Widespread but localised in southern Britain, usually in woods and by heaths.

BLACK REDSTART

Phoenicurus ochruros

In Britain confined to industrial sites and the urban jungle, but in the rest of Europe most likely to be seen on rocky hillsides.

Identification Robin-like but slimmer, males are all black with rufous tail; females a greyish brown, also showing rufous on tail. Darker than Common Redstart.

Habits Males often sing from high building or perch on industrial machinery. On continent more likely to perch on rocks.

Feeding & breeding
Feeds on small invertebrates and some fruit. Breeds in hole in wall or building.

Voice Quiet, fairly rapid warble, reminiscent of ball bearings being clattered together.

When & where Partial migrant, often wintering at lower altitudes or near coasts. Common throughout continental Europe, and a few pairs in southern Britain including central London!

FIRECREST

Regulus ignicapillus

Marginally bigger than its commoner cousin the Goldcrest, and more likely to be seen in mixed or deciduous woodland.

Identification Tiny, bright little bird. Told apart from Goldcrest by black eyestripe, more fiery crown, whiter wing bars, and obvious orange patch on flanks.

Habits Like Goldcrest, flicks around leaves of trees to glean insects, often hovering momentarily to do so.

Feeding & breeding Feeds on tiny insects. Builds tiny nest suspended from end of twigs or leaves.

Voice Song series of high-pitched repeated notes, lacking rhythm of Goldcrest. Call, a high-pitched 'zit'.

When & where Partial migrant, found breeding throughout continental Europe. Rare breeder in southern Britain; also sometimes seen on migration and in winter, especially near the coast.

SHORT-TOED TREECREEPER
Certhia brachydactyla

The southern and western counterpart of the Treecreeper is almost impossible to identify with certainty in the field, and as a result may have been overlooked in Britain.

Identification Very similar to Treecreeper, and only told apart with certainty in the hand. Slightly longer bill and browner flanks. Best identified by geographical location or with practice, by its song.

Habits Like the Treecreeper, spends most of its life crawling around the trunks and branches of trees in search of tiny insects.

Feeding & breeding Feeds on tiny invertebrates and their grubs, obtained with its sharp, decurved bill.

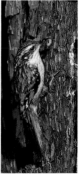

Voice Similar to Treecreeper, but louder and more forceful.

When & where Resident in suitable wooded habitat throughout southern and western Europe. Very rare vagrant to southern Britain.

GOLDEN ORIOLE

Oriolus oriolus

This stunning but shy bird rarely reveals its presence, apart from its distinctive and fluty song.

Identification Male unmistakable: bright golden-yellow plumage with red bill and black wings. Female much less bright, overall greenish yellow with pale greyish underparts.

Habits Skulks high in foliage of trees, rarely revealing its presence apart from when it flies, showing its gaudy plumage.

Feeding & breeding Feeds on insects, especially caterpillars. Breeds high in tall trees, building its nest from grass in a tree fork.

Voice A lyrical and fluty series of four notes: 'wee-la-wee-ooo' – once heard, never forgotten.

When & where Summer visitor to much of continental Europe south of Scandinavia, though rarely seen well. Breeds in small numbers in eastern Britain, usually in conifer plantations.

HOODED CROW

Corvus cornix

Recently 'split' from its more familiar relative the Carrion Crow, this species has an unusual and fragmented distribution across Europe.

Identification The only large crow with substantial areas of grey on plumage: black head and wings contrast with rest of plumage.

Habits Like all crows, highly adaptable and opportunistic, often hanging around human habitation to see what it can get!

Feeding & breeding Omnivorous, taking all kinds of food where available, including invertebrates and grain. Breeds in tree or occasionally on cliff or rock.

Voice Loud, raucous cawing sound, usually uttered in flight.

When & where Mainly found in eastern and northern Europe, including the far north and west of Scotland and the whole of Ireland. Rare visitor to southern Scotland, England and Wales. Resident.

SERIN

Serinus serinus

This tiny finch is a common garden bird all over continental Europe, but despite several attempts, has yet to establish a foothold as a British breeding bird. Climate change may alter all that, however.

Identification A tiny greenish-yellow bird, with a round head, short forked tail and streaky plumage.

Habits Usually sings from a prominent post such as bush or telegraph wire. Often found in gardens and villages.

Feeding & breeding Feeds on small insects including caterpillars. Breeds in dense foliage of bush or tree.

Voice A distinctive jangling song, quite like that of Corn Bunting.

When & where Partial migrant, found throughout continental Europe. Annual visitor to southern England, usually in spring. Has bred in Devon and Dorset, and may well do so again.

INDEX OF SPECIES